Christian Philosophy in the Early Church

Christian Philosophy in the Early Church

By

Anthony Meredith S.J.

t&t clark

Published by T&T Clark International

A Continuum Imprint

The Tower Building	80 Maiden Lane
11 York Road	Suite 704
London	New York
SE1 7NX	NY 10038

www.continuumbooks.com

British Library Cataloguing-in-Publication Data

A catalogue record for this book is available from the British Library

ISBN: 978-0-5672-7860-9 (hardback)
978-0-5673-0818-4 (paperback)

Typeset by Deanta Global Publishing Services, Chennai, India
Printed and bound in India

CONTENTS

1

Introduction

The Christian religion was born in and into first century Palestine. When exactly it began is not altogether clear. Was it at the moment of the Incarnation, or was it on the cross with the piercing of the side of Christ as recorded in the fourth gospel (19.34), or was it with the descent of the Holy Spirit on the Apostles in the upper room as recorded in the opening chapters of the Acts of the Apostles? For the purposes of the ensuing study it hardly matters which particular moment is accepted. All were historical moments. They all occurred in Roman occupied Palestine between the beginning of our era and about the year 30 AD.

Jesus Christ was a Jew, and so too were his family and closest followers. The first followers and hearers of Jesus were not drawn from the intellectual and social elite of their day, but rather from artisans, tax collectors and the more disreputable members of society. Yet out of such seemingly unpromising and insignificant beginnings, a seed was planted by his teaching, his cross and resurrection, which was destined to spread its shade over the entire known world. What had begun life as an essentially Jewish movement founded on the preaching, life, death and resurrection of the Messiah from Nazareth became, by an astonishing and even now quite mysterious process and with quite amazing speed, a religion that was accepted not only by Jews and proselytes but also by pagans, Goths, Franks and eventually by the New World.

No one has so far offered an adequate historical explanation of the reasons for this astonishing success story. The appeal of the presence and action of the Holy Spirit at its beginning on the first Whit Sunday is no doubt the ultimate secret, but such a reason is not enough to satisfy the historian. All we can do is to trace its path, mapped out by the hurrying footsteps of the divine apostle Saint Paul, among others, who was above all responsible for the transformation of an essentially Jewish movement into a more universal faith. But this transformation was not only spatial; it also affected its self understanding. As we shall see, it would be overly facile to speak of a violent break with the Jewish roots of the church.

This is partly because the roots were never purely Jewish in the sense of what was later understood as Rabbinic Judaism. The Palestine into which Jesus was born in the first century AD was not 'uncontaminated' by alien wisdom. Part of Jesus' own mission took place in the Greek speaking Decapolis region.[1] Further to that, Greek interest in Jesus is strongly suggested by the Greeks who 'wanted to see Jesus'.[2] It is unlikely that the subsequent discussion was conducted in Hebrew or Aramaic.

This means that within Palestinian Jewry, the attempt had already started to relate to a wider audience well before Christianity stepped into the shoes of Judaism. The use, therefore, made by later Christian writers of ideas and language drawn from the culture of the day, was simply an extension both of the initial dynamism of the gospel and an attempt to render real the final words of Jesus as they appear in Saint Matthew's gospel to 'go and teach all nations'.[3] The conversion and subsequent mission of Saint Paul[4] reminds us that Paul was designated 'Apostle of the Gentiles' 'to carry my name before Gentiles and Kings' from an early date. The need for an interpretative tool with which to recommend the good news was evident from the very beginning of the enterprise. Language is the vehicle through which the gospel was transmitted, and if it was to be understood, it was not enough simply to repeat the exact words and language of the Master. It stood in need of both translation and at a later date also of interpretation if it was to be intelligible and appealing to all.

Facing the problem

At the outset, therefore, we are faced with certain problems of definition, without attending to which the ensuing discussion will be in danger of drifting into obscurity. Unfortunately however, the terms requiring definition are not at all easy to define, as we shall

---

[1] Mk 7.31.
[2] Jn 12.20-22.
[3] Mt. 28.19.
[4] Acts 9.15.

see. To begin with we need to ask ourselves the question 'what is the essence of Christianity?' Has Christianity got a definable essence at all? Is it at all possible to arrive at a definition of Christianity agreed on by all, with which to contrast various attempts to structure the gospel message with the aid of philosophy? Was the gospel's concern with orthopraxy, that is, doing the right thing, or was it orthodoxy, that is, the importance of truth in religion, as subsequently articulated and insisted on by the Church through the creeds?

Again, does the word 'Christianity' itself mean quite the same in the first and the fourth centuries? How fair was Edwin Hatch to mark a distinction[5] between the moral stress of the Sermon on the Mount and the combination of both history and metaphysical ideas embedded in the creeds of Nicaea (in 325 AD) and Constantinople (in 381 CE). Shortly before Hatch's essay appeared, Matthew Arnold had taken an even bolder step and endeavoured to reduce all factual elements in the gospel to moral ideas. Arnold writes: 'the true meaning of religion is thus, not simply *morality*, but *morality touched by emotion*'.[6]

In the same way, towards the end of the nineteenth century, Adolf von Harnack proposed a celebrated definition of Christianity as 'the Fatherhood of God, the brotherhood of man, and the infinite value of the human soul'.[7] He regarded metaphysics, which in his view began to infiltrate into Christianity from the middle of the second century together with a priestly and monastic system, as alien growths on the soil of the gospel. Although his views have not met with uncritical acceptance, his words have proved a beacon for those who have explored the subject of the supposed hellenization of the gospel ever since.

But was his definition as satisfactory as it has certainly proved challenging? Was Holl, another German theologian, fair to insist against von Harnack that the sinfulness of man and his need of grace was at the heart of the gospel? The search for a definition of the essence of Christianity is by and large a Protestant preoccupation and has obvious advantages as it enables one to discover what is and what is not essential to faith. Richard Field, an Anglican

---

[5] As he does at the opening of his Hibbert Lectures for 1888 entitled, 'The Influence of Greek Ideas and Usages upon the Christian Church'.
[6] M. Arnold, *Literature and Dogma* (1873, 1906), p. 16, italics in the original.
[7] A. von Harnack, *The Essence of Christianity* (1900–1). Karl Holl (1866–1926).

dean of Gloucester in the early years of the seventeenth century, argued for a distinction between primary and secondary articles of faith.[8] But is such a distinction justified? A more general and less precise approach that concentrates on the double command to love God and our neighbour is preferable, leaving the working out to development in both areas.

One important factor that serves to unite Jews and Christians is that for all of them, the knowledge of the Supreme Being was mediated primarily above all in sacred books. Revelation comes primarily through a historical revelation and therefore in history. The exodus from Egyptian captivity for the Jews, and the life, death and resurrection of Jesus Christ were all historical and at the same time defining moments, carefully recorded in sacred texts.

For the Greeks by contrast, even before the advent of the pre-Socratics, the gods were thought of as expressions of physical and moral truths, not as historical figures: Zeus was the sky god and Hera goddess of the air. The appeal then and later was rather to nature and the moral law – the starry heavens above and the moral law within. The poems of Homer: *The Iliad* and *The Odyssey*, though to some extent regarded as the bible of the Greeks, were not perceived to be accurate accounts of the behaviour of the gods. Plato in his *Republic* thought their influence sufficiently pernicious in their account of the behaviour of the gods that he wished to forbid them to be recited in his ideal state.

It is true of course that certain passages in the psalms, for example the opening of Psalm 19, 'The heavens declare the glory of God', reflect a more positive attitude to natural theology than a sharp dichotomy might suggest. Nevertheless Exodus,[9] Deuteronomy,[10] the Psalms and Isaiah[11] portray God as the personal creator and lord of the universe. For the Christian the supreme revelation of God is to be found in Jesus of Nazareth. To the idea of the divine supremacy, so prominent in the Old Testament, the New Testament adds the revelation of God as love.[12]

---

[8]R. Field, *Of the Church*, (Cambridge University Press, 1847).
[9]Especially the experience of Exod. 3.14.
[10]Especially Deut. 6.4, 'The Lord is our God, the Lord alone'.
[11]Especially Isa. 45.18 ff, 'For thus says the Lord, who created the heavens (he is God), who formed the earth (he established it, he did not create it a chaos, he formed it to be inhabited!) "I am the Lord and there is no other"'.
[12]1 Jn 4.8.

The question immediately arises as to the possibility of harmonizing these two accounts of the ultimate reality, the natural and the revealed, and the different routes that lead to them. Can reason and revelation be brought into harmony with each other, linking nature, morality and history? To this important question Christians have from the outset proposed very different replies. Some of these will be discussed in Chapter 2. One of the most celebrated answers is that offered by Blaise Paschal. In a moment of revelation on 23 November in the year of grace 1654, he begins his *Pensées* with the celebrated words: '"God of Abraham, God of Isaac, God of Jacob" not of philosophers and scholars'.[13] At a later date, Professor Kneale in the course of a lecture insisted that the idea of a personal absolute was, at least for him, a contradiction in terms.[14]

Again how could a being that is beyond the reach of both change and moral variability be also compassionate and incarnate? Perhaps more importantly, does the thought of what is fitting for God to be and do stand in judgement upon the data of biblical revelation? Gregory of Nyssa insists that the Christian concept of God must include the four basic ideas of justice, wisdom, goodness and power.[15] Does one have to choose between rationalism and some form, biblical or ecclesial, of fundamentalism? Is the philosophic idea always in danger of ousting the biblical idea? Writers from Plato onwards have argued that the highest human ideals of goodness, justice, wisdom and power must also be realized in our understanding of the divine nature. The divine credibility is measured by his moral character.

It is therefore by no means self evident that there exists a harmonious unity between two such very distinct approaches. Personality and absolute being are not natural soul mates. As we shall see, the need for this connection or identification of the two, far from being a Christian innovation, had already been advocated by some of the later disciples of Plato. They also seem to have wanted to build a bridge between the philosophy and the religion of the Greeks in a way quite distinct from the non-religious philosophy of Plato and Plotinus. And this liaison was also affirmed by the great Christian philosophical tradition begun by Justin and deepened by Origen, Augustine and Thomas Aquinas who saw in God both

---

[13]Paschal, *Pensées*, (Penguin, 2003), p. 285.
[14]Professor Kneale in a lecture in Oxford.
[15]Gregory of Nyssa, *Catechetical Oration*, Chapter. 19.

the personal being of the bible and the mental construct of the philosophers.

The four great Christian writers just mentioned were men of great intellectual power but also believers and men of prayer: one of them, Justin, was a martyr and Origen was eager to become one. Were they being beguiled into supposing that the alliance between the believer's adhesion to a personal being and the philosophic ideas of the good or the One was possible? Or were they in the right?

Faith and philosophy: Alliance or hostility?

'Christian theology', wrote the German classical scholar, Albrecht Dihle, 'is an attempt to make intelligible with the help of philosophy the biblical texts about the Creator and Father God, the Sonship of Jesus and his humanity, and the work of the Holy Spirit. The philosophy of later antiquity', he continues 'was Platonism, a philosophy of being and its eternal order climaxing in God'.[16] Dihle's point is that Plato provided the key for the better understanding of the basic facts of revelation, as they are enshrined in the primary documents of the Christian faith, above all in the four gospels and the letters of Saint Paul. At the beginning of his 1998 encyclical *Fides et Ratio*, Pope John Paul II made a similar claim when he stated that: 'Faith and reason seem to be like two wings by which the human spirit is raised upward toward the contemplation of the truth'.[17]

Both reason and revelation emanate from the same divine source. There ought not, therefore, to be a chasm between the two. Basing himself on the Septuagint version of Isa. 7.9 'Unless you believe you will not understand', Saint Augustine argued that 'faith seeks understanding' at the end of Book vii of his *On the Trinity*. So he writes:

> There must be neither confusing nor mixing up of the persons [sc. of the Trinity] nor such distinction of them as may imply

---

[16]Albrecht Dihle (1982), p. 51. *The theory of will in Classical Antiquity* – Sather Classical Lectures 1982.
[17]Pope John Paul II, *Fides et ratio*.

disparity. If this cannot be grasped by understanding, let it be held by faith, until he shines in our minds who said by the prophet "Unless you believe you will not understand".[18]

Augustine's translator Edmund Hill notes: 'This is probably his favourite quotation'.[19] At a later date, Saint Anselm (1033–1109) exploited the same text for the same purpose. At the end of the opening prayer of his *Proslogion*, Anselm concludes: 'I do not seek to understand so that I may believe, but I believe so that I may understand; and what is more, I believe that unless I do believe I shall not understand'.[20]

The primary aim of what follows is historical. Its purpose is less to justify the actual fact of philosophic influence than to illustrate the truth of the claim that in fact the church has been influenced by philosophy, and that this did not begin once the church felt confident enough to express itself in language not specifically biblical, but from its earliest records, above all the letters of Saint Paul. This aim will be realized by examining the various relationships that have in fact existed between Christian faith and secular philosophy at least in the course of the first five centuries of the history of the church.

The second aim is more apologetic. It endeavours to defend the actual presence within Christian belief of a large measure of philosophical input. It hopes to explore the light that may be thrown on the nature of Christian belief by such an inquiry, and in so doing it poses the following question: is it possible to have a deliberately non-philosophical faith, that is to say a faith that expresses its meaning without the help of philosophy? If the gospel of Christ is meant to recommend itself to the mind as well as to the heart and will, so the argument runs, it ought to be possible to appreciate something of its meaning with the help of philosophical spectacles. To relapse into unthinking fideism is to play into the hands of the cultured despisers of the gospel from Celsus[21] in the second century onwards.

A further question arises once it is admitted that philosophy has a role to play in the articulation of the gospel. Is it possible to

---

[18] Augustine, *On the Trinity*, 7, 12 and 15.2.
[19] p. 236. New City Press 1991.
[20] Anselm, *Proslogion*, (Penguin Classics) p. 244.
[21] Origen reports Celsus as saying that certain Christians of his time 'use such expressions as "Do not ask questions; just believe"' (*Contra Celsum*, 1.9).

discover a formula which helps to distinguish between a correct and an incorrect, that is a heretical, use of philosophy? Origen, for example clearly used philosophy and yet not only was he censured, at least for some of his views three hundred years or more after his death in 254 AD, he was also conscious of the 'threat' posed to faith by philosophy. Towards the close of his seventh *Homily on Joshua*, Origen warns his congregation against the gold found in Jericho that was, he argues, the source of the heretical opinions of the Gnostics Valentinus, Basilides and Marcion. It is quaint to find Origen censuring others for precisely the mistakes of which he himself was accused. Is there a connexion between these two faces of Origen – the philosopher and the anti-philosopher? Is the difference to be found simply in the nature of the audience he was addressing?

As will become clearer, it is not always easy to discover the leading motive in the works of a given author. Arius, often thought of as the arch-heretic, is a case in point: does he represent a deliberate attempt to rewrite or revise the creed of his day in a more authentically biblical fashion or is he a middle Platonist philosopher at heart, a philosophical wolf in the dress of a Christian sheep as Professor Stead[22] and many others have argued? The respective roles played by faith and reason are not always easy to disentangle.

One of the intriguing features to emerge from this investigation is that although it is relatively common to accuse one's opponents of allowing themselves to be seduced by philosophy, it is unusual for scholars to accuse each other of fundamentalism or literalism in their attitude to the bible. Although this needs a little qualification in the light of Origen's allegorical defence of the bible against the literalism of Marcion[23] and Gregory of Nyssa's critique of the methods of Eunomius.[24] For both Origen and Gregory, what was missing in the works of their opponents was a more refined approach to the meaning of the bible. All early Christian writers without exception offer their views with the aid of a large scriptural dress. Why was this the case and does an investigation of the surviving evidence justify the conclusion that as a basis for Christian belief, 'biblicism'

---

[22]C. Stead, *Divine Substance*, (Oxford University Press, 1977).

[23]Origen, *On First Principles*, Book 4, 2:2.

[24]Gregory of Nyssa and the connection between Eunomius and Aristotle in *Contra Eunomium* 1, 46; 2, 411; 3, 5:6 and 3, 10:50.

is in order but philosophy is not? Is faith equivalently an acceptance of the literal truth of the bible or is it something else?

The missionary character of Christianity

One of the respects in which Christianity differed from its parent was in its essentially missionary character. It is of course true that Isaiah looked forward to a time when 'my house shall be a house of prayer for all peoples'[25] and there were also many proselytes who formed a nucleus of future Jews round the synagogue.[26] Even so, it would be misleading to describe Judaism as a missionary faith, especially by comparison with Christianity and Islam. It was essentially a national religion and in that respect less strange to the Greeks and Romans than was Christianity with its more universal outreach.

Adult male converts to Judaism would have to undergo a painful operation if they were to be admitted. Paul had to insist principally in his *Letter to the Galatians* that the gospel was for all and that membership of the new faith did not make the same sort of demands upon its neophytes as did the Jews. Even Paul was not entirely consistent in the matter as we are told that 'he had Timothy circumcised because of the Jews that were in those places'.[27]

On the whole, both then and now, most Jews are born so, Christians, however, by contrast in the words of a later writer Tertullian: 'were not so born, but became so'[28] – an expression later exploited by Saint Jerome nearly two centuries later in 403.[29] It is perhaps worth noting here that there is no evidence of missionary zeal among the Greeks either. Greek city states and the colonies they founded were markedly self-enclosed and made no attempt to spread their culture outside themselves.

---

[25]Isa. 56.7.
[26]Acts 13.43.
[27]Acts 16.3.
[28]Apology 18.4.
[29]In letter 107.

There is nothing in Judaism or Hellenism to equal the final charge of Jesus at the end of Saint Matthew's gospel to go 'and teach all nations'.[30] Judaism never produced a missionary like Saint Paul whose hurrying footsteps 'in journeyings often'[31] carried the good news of Jesus Christ right over the northern coasts of the eastern Mediterranean. But how? How did he manage to recommend his message to the people who listened to him? What sort of audience did he find? What sort of culture did he meet? What concessions, if any, did he make to the Hellenic culture he met in Thessalonica, Athens and Corinth?

Continuity with Jewish faith

Christianity inherited a Jewish God and a Jewish covenant. It is true that the continuity of the God of the Old Testament with the Father of Our Lord Jesus Christ did not seem to everybody a self evident truth. Saint Paul's insistence upon it, above all when he says that Abraham is the 'father of all believers',[32] rather more than suggests that not everybody was happy with the implied continuity. And in the second century, as we have already seen, one of the most powerful and suggestive thinkers of the early church, Marcion, denied the identity of the two and rejected or tried to remove the Old Testament and a large part of the New from the cadre of the bible, leaving behind only an emasculated Luke and a revised Paul.

God of Old Testament versus God of New Testament

There is much truth in the assertion that the God whom the Jews worshipped was essentially and irreducibly personal. As such he was adored and prayed to usually in the second person singular, though apparently, not until the arrival of the gospel was he addressed in prayer as Father, a fact noted by Origen.[33] This God was essentially

---

[30]Mt. 28.19-20.
[31]2 Cor. 11.26
[32]In Chapter 4 of the *Letter to the Romans*.
[33]His treatise *On Prayer*, Chapter 22.

a historical being, who acted and revealed himself in and through history. He was also an emotional being, who could be both angry and merciful, and he is sometimes described as a jealous God unwilling to share his worship with another. He is also active and favours one particular nation: all this we can learn from the book of Exodus, above all in chs 6 and 20, while the books of Joshua and Judges and some of the Psalms, above all the vengeful Psalms 82 and 108, make very unpleasant reading to a more sophisticated readership.

Jewish worship versus Greek idolatry

The Greeks in their religion appealed above all to the sense of sight. Some of the beautiful statues of their gods and goddesses still survive. The Jews, by contrast, were without images of the divine. Making images of God was expressly forbidden. Exodus reads 'You shall not make to yourself a graven image or any likeness of anything that is in heaven above or in the earth beneath'.[34] This clearly puzzled the Romans when they sacked the temple in 70 AD.[35] The Jews appealed rather to the sense of hearing: 'Hear, O Israel'. Magnificent though the temple was, it did not invite the worshippers of the Lord to gaze on a picture of God or on his statue. Josephus likewise reports the resistance of the Jews to the setting up of an image of the emperor in the temple and 'explained that it was not permissible for a graven image of God, much less of man to be placed in the temple'.[36]

Jewish morality versus Jewish ritualism

The Jewish religion, above all in its prophetic side, concentrated on the moral as distinct from the ritualistic and speculative aspects of religion. Isaiah censures the Jews for their attention to ritual obligations and their corresponding neglect of the needs of the poor:

---

[34]Exod. 20.4.
[35]Tacitus, *Histories*, book V.
[36]Josephus, *The Jewish War*, book 2, Section 200.

Is not this the fast that I choose: to loose the bonds of wickedness, to undo the thongs of the yoke, to let the oppressed go free and to break every yoke? Is it not to share your bread with the hungry, and bring the homeless poor into your house; when you see the naked, to cover him, and not to hide yourself from your own flesh?[37]

Need for charity/pedagogy – service to society – political connections

The Decalogue, especially in its final six precepts, is essentially a series of moral commands regulating our relationships to one another. It is true that in its opening commands it enjoins the worship of and obedience to God, but it assumes the existence of God and the need to offer him worship, while offering no rational account of his nature. Again, although the Decalogue may not differ much in *content* from natural law, its dictates are commands not suggestions from God and are not simply the result of human prudence. Coming as they do from the same God, hardly surprisingly, the natural law of Plato and the Stoics is in large a measure of agreement with the Ten Commandments. A comparison between Ezekiel's vision of God recorded in Chapter 1 of his *Prophecy* and the vision of the idea of the good described by Plato in books 6 and 7 of the *Republic* is instructive. Both are to issue in action, neither vision is simply to be enjoyed for itself. But whereas the vision of the prophet seems to be gratuitous and not to result from previous mental activity, that of Plato is a direct result of moral and intellectual seriousness.

The difference between the action-oriented approach of the bible and that of the Greeks is clear and instructive but easy to exaggerate. Although it is true that the Pre-Socratic philosophers seem to have been primarily interested in exploring the structure of the physical universe, the Sophists were above all concerned with behaviour. Plato's search for absolute goodness was also undertaken for a moral purpose, and the search for it demanded moral as well as intellectual seriousness. But for Plato, at least in the *Republic*,

---

[37] 2 Isaiah 58.

speculation is not thought of as an end in itself. In book 7 of the *Republic* we find one of the few invitations to set aside one's own intellectual satisfaction for the sake of the other citizens. Plato writes 'one must descend for a while'.[38] In other words the quest for absolute truth was not undertaken simply to satisfy one's own mental curiosity, but in order that one may be of important service to society at large. It had an essentially political orientation. It is also worth noting that the actual moral recommendations of Plato and precepts of Moses are not very unlike each other.

As we shall see, Plato's pupil Aristotle adopted a rather different approach. Aristotle's death in 322 BC coincided with the absorption of Athens into the world empire of Philip of Macedon and of his son Alexander the Great. With the decline of the importance of the individual, the motive of political interest becomes correspondingly less prominent.

The challenge of and to the gospel

Christianity from its outset, as preserved for us in the writings of the New Testament, presents us with several apparently unavoidable tensions. First, one we commonly gloss over, the distance between the Old and New Testaments and the differing images of God they disclose. Something of this will be discussed in the next section on the Jewish background. But we should not try to obscure the fact that the Old Testament God is, among other qualities, a just God and also one who is jealous. We read: 'I, the Lord your God am a jealous God, visiting the iniquity of the fathers upon the children to the third and fourth generation of those that hate me'.[39]

The God and Father of Jesus Christ, though just, is also, and more importantly, merciful and not vindictive, except perhaps, in Revelation. He invites his followers to 'be merciful even as your Father is merciful'.[40] The distance that separates Old and New Covenants is considerable. The central message of the divine mercy, of the kingdom of God, and the crucifixion and resurrection of the Son of God seem quite alien to the Old Testament. It is hardly

---

[38] Plato, *Republic*, book 7, 420c.
[39] Exod. 20.4.
[40] Lk. 6.36.

surprising that Christian writers, like Marcion at the beginning of the second century, proposed a complete break between the two covenants. How, he reasoned, could the God who ordered the destruction of Ai[41] be the very same being as the one who in the Sermon on the Mount in the person of his Son said: 'I say to you, love your enemies and pray for those who persecute you'.[42] It took the genius of Origen to provide an answer to this formidable challenge, and in so doing preserve both the fourfold gospel and the Old Testament for the church.

The second tension arises from the fact that it is indeed true that Christianity is emphatically a historical faith, with roots in a particular place and time – first century Palestine under Roman occupation. Pontius Pilate, the centurions we meet in the gospels, and the tax collectors or publicans were agents of hated Roman domination. Being a historical reality it contains of necessity elements of contingency and freedom. In other words we could ask, as we can of any historical event, did it have to be so? Jesus of Nazareth was a historical figure, whose words and deeds are preserved for us above all in the four gospels. But were the actual circumstances of his coming into this world and his departure from it accidental?

On the other hand, from the earliest times he was also perceived to be more than a historical figure and was greeted as Lord and God. So in the Prologue of the fourth gospel, he is the Word and the Word was God'[43] and he is worshipped by Thomas the apostle as 'My Lord and my God'.[44] In two of the letters of Saint Paul, both dating from the sixties of the first century, if not earlier, similar claims are advanced, so we read: 'No one says Jesus is Lord save in the Holy Spirit'[45] and 'Jesus is Lord'.[46]

He was a divine being accorded a divine title, and being divine, he was outside and independent of both time and history. His importance to us and the weight we attach to his moral teaching derives both from its inherent nobility but also from the fact of his being the Son of God. The eternal and temporal meet in Christ,

---

[41]'You shall do to Ai and its king what you did to Jericho' Josh. 8.2.
[42]Mt. 5.44.
[43]Jn 1.3.
[44]Jn 20.28.
[45]I Cor. 12.3.
[46]In the hymn at Phil. 2.11.

as they do in no other single person. If this is true and a Christian assents to it in the Creed, we are faced with a challenging mystery. For, if this claim is true, it will compel us to revise our understanding of the nature of both God and man.

It was to the exploration and resolution of this seeming paradox that much of the early history of Christianity was devoted. History finds it hard to do justice to any individual and Christ was unique not only as all people are, but in the further sense that in the Nicene Creed affirmed at Nicaea in 325 and reaffirmed in a slightly expanded form in 381, the Christian confesses him to be God from God in a quite unique fashion.

The third and final tension lies in the fact that it was not and is not easy to do justice to Jesus' mysterious character. There had never been and there has never been anyone quite like him. If it be asked 'could the church have come to any other answer than she did about his person and nature?' the answer is both yes and no. The Creed of Nicaea of 325 could not have been otherwise in the sense that it enunciates an absolute truth. Yet the journey to Nicaea was hazardous and by no means self evident. The emperor Constantine summoned the council, and without his initiative nothing would have been defined. Athanasius needed to fight for the truth of the creed. Its truth was not self evident to all Christians. There is therefore a twofold contingency at work here. Christ as man was part of the world of change and contingency. The church as being both a human and divine reality, like its head, displays both necessary and contingent elements in its composition and these are inextricably connected.

A further question at once surfaces: How was it possible for the new faith, with its unique blend of time and eternity, to be both Jewish and missionary at the same time; to make converts from the world into which it was inserted and yet remain true to its largely Jewish roots? Would it be enough for the earliest messengers of the kingdom simply to 'translate' the message into Greek, the lingua franca of the empire and offer no attempt at enculturation? The only solid evidence we have of the actual tactics of the early preachers outside the Holy Land itself is to be found in Acts and in the *Letters* of Saint Paul. But even Paul, who in the *First Letter to the Corinthians* launched a sort of diatribe against the value of the philosophy of this world, was prepared to use ideas taken from it, above all in the first and second chapters of his *Letter to the Romans*.

True zeal must begin from where the audience is and then proceed to bring it further. We find Saint Paul doing exactly this in his speech at Athens.[47] The church was compelled to provide an overarching canvass into which her beliefs about God and Christ could fit. Hostile critics both then and now wished to treat Christianity as a religion intended solely for the simple and ill-educated, with a motto of 'Only believe'. Jesus himself was brought up as a carpenter; his closest followers were fisherman. Saint Paul was by trade a tent maker.[48] Yet despite the fact that Jesus himself never left Palestine, his gospel had a worldwide message.[49] This is more than hinted at in his lifetime by his encounters with the Magi[50] and the Greeks.[51]

The Jewish background

We should not forget that the cradle in which the gospel was born was essentially Jewish. Jesus himself was a Jew, as were his mother Mary and his foster father Joseph. He was circumcised when eight days old.[52] He was found by his anxious parents in the temple when only twelve, arguing with the doctors of the law.[53] His first sermon was delivered, according to Saint Luke, in a synagogue in his home town of Nazareth.[54] He rarely left the country of his birth and upbringing, though, as we have seen, he probably could speak Greek. All his disciples and friends were Jews as were his enemies. Yet even the Infancy narratives give a hint of the more universal outreach of the gospel. The Wise men came from the east[55] and the words of aged Simeon describe him as a 'light to enlighten the gentiles'.[56]

---

[47]Acts 17.
[48]Acts 18.3.
[49]Mt. 28.19.
[50]Matthew. 2.
[51]John 12.
[52]Lk. 2.21.
[53]Lk. 2.46.
[54]Lk. 4.16.
[55]Mt. 2.1.
[56]Lk. 2.32.

The narrative of his journey through Samaria in Chapter 4 of the fourth gospel is a good example of the divisions existing in first century Palestine among those who were in many respects very close in their beliefs. It was not customary for good Jews to have any contact with their Samaritan neighbours, whom they regarded as quislings of a once hostile power. We hear occasionally of other encounters with non-Jews,[57] but his mission was primarily and almost exclusively to 'the lost sheep of the house of Israel'.[58] His dialogue with Pontius Pilate during his cross examination was conducted almost certainly without the help of an interpreter. But the sermons he preached and the miracles he worked show him using Aramaic or spoken Hebrew. A few words of Aramaic or spoken Hebrew are preserved for us by Mark, 'talitha cum'[59] to the little girl, the daughter of Jairus which means 'Little girl, I say to you arise'. His word to the deaf mute 'Ephphetha'[60] simply means 'Be opened'.

And what is true of the founder was true also of the first missionaries. It appears from the Acts of the Apostles that initial apostolic enterprise took place in Judaea and in synagogues. The early Christians continued to worship in the temple,[61] but even so, we need not assume that the only language available or actually used was Aramaic. Greek was certainly in use in the Decapolis region and one of the Apostles at least, Philip, had a Greek name and it was to him that the Greeks addressed themselves when they came to him with the request 'We should like to see Jesus'.[62]

Although, therefore, there were distinct differences between the native Jews and the Greeks, it is misleading to suggest that there was a clear cultural barrier between the two. This is important as it helps to explain how a predominantly Jewish faith was able to recommend and explain its message to the outside world, or rather to the world outside Palestine. Even so certain traditional approaches that underline the gap between Judaism and the surrounding Hellenistic world need pointing out, partly in order to highlight the challenge faced by the universal mission of the early church.

---

[57] Like the centurion in John 4 and the Syrophoenician woman in Mark 7.
[58] Mt. 15.24.
[59] Mk 5.41.
[60] Mk 7.34.
[61] As we learn from Acts 2 and 4.
[62] Jn 12.20.

The Greek and Hellenistic background

Before, therefore, the relationship between the two basic elements – the bible and philosophy – is entered upon, it is of some importance to be clear about the cultural milieu which encountered the early church and the philosophical options open to nascent Christianity. The first point has been very stimulatingly explored by Keith Hopkins in his *A World Full of Gods*[63] in which he helps to explain the sharp challenges presented to the early believers in a diverse and in many ways rather crude society. There may have been, as Saint Paul tells us, 'Gods many and lords many'[64] but, as Plato long before had reminded his readers,[65] many of them were far from being paragons of virtue. Gods like Zeus, Mars, Apollo and Bacchus and semi-gods like Heracles seem to have had only one purpose in life, to make love to as many girls and pretty boys as they could seduce.

The poets

Among the earliest records of Greek civilization, above all in the works of the poets Homer, Aeschylus and Sophocles, there is an acknowledgement of the existence of a supreme personal being (beings) who exercises absolute control over human affairs. At the very outset of the *Iliad* we read that in and through the often refractory wills of obstinate mortals 'the purpose of Zeus was accomplished'.[66] To the outward eye it may look as though the wrath of Achilles was responsible for all, but in fact God was in control. And at the close of the *Iliad*, when Achilles is to meet Priam, we read that the gods have allotted to men their respective destinies.[67] Are we really a long way from Augustine who writes: 'therefore that God, the author and giver of all happiness, because he alone is the true God, Himself gives both good and bad to earthly kingdoms'?[68] The issues of divine providence and human responsibility are never

[63]K. Hopkins, *A World Full of Gods*, (Weidenfeld & Nicholson, 1999).
[64]1 Cor. 8.5.
[65]Plato, *Republic*, book 4.
[66]Homer, *Iliad*, i. 5.
[67]Homer, *Iliad*, 24: 525.
[68]Augustine, *City of God* 4: 33.

far away. The divine apparatus that surrounds them may differ, but the relationship of god(s) and men is the central theme. The difficulty lies in disentangling the two.

Aeschylus also, in language strangely reminiscent of the words of the *Magnificat*,[69] can write that 'Zeus is the chastiser of overweening pride'.[70] It is above all in his greatest play, *The Agamemnon*, that the power of Zeus to control events is most seriously stated. On three separate occasions the control of God is emphasized by the chorus. On the first of these, the chorus exclaims 'Zeus who leads mortals in the way of understanding and who has established as a fixed ordinance that "wisdom comes by suffering"'.[71] And later the chorus argues that the hand of Zeus may be traced in the disaster of Troy: 'Now stands revealed how ruin is the penalty for reckless crime, when men breathe a spirit of pride'.[72] Finally towards the close of the play, shortly after the murder by Clytemnestra of Agamemnon and the prophetess Cassandra, the chorus cries out '[All comes about] by the will of Zeus, author of all, worker of all! For what is brought to pass for mortal men save by the will of Zeus? What is there that is not wrought by heaven?' What appears to the outward eye to be the result of the wills of men is in fact brought about through the divine will. The effort to reconcile human freedom and divine providence was not therefore a peculiarly Christian problem.

Similarly, the tragedies of Sophocles, above all his greatest *Oedipus Rex*, offer a powerful commentary on the ultimate frailty of human nature in the face of the mysterious designs of God. Oedipus struggles to avert the doom revealed by the oracle before his birth of killing his father, Laius, and marrying his mother Jocasta and, ironically, he fails in his attempt, precisely because he has done all he could to avoid his dreadful fate. The power of God is less stressed here, where the accent falls more on human psychology and frailty than it does in Aeschylus. The ending of the tragedy is a sad lament on the uncertainty of human fate, with the refrain 'call no man happy before death'. The oracle of Apollo may not be

---

[69]'He has put down the mighty from their thrones and exalted those of low degree' Lk. 1.52.
[70]Aeschylus, *The Persians*, 827.
[71]Aeschylus, *The Agamemnon*, 173 ff.
[72]Aeschylus, *The Agamemnon*, 366.

evaded. Oedipus himself cries out 'It was Apollo that brought these my woes to pass, these my sore, sore woes'.[73]

In a later play, *The Philoctetes*, it is the hero's patron Heracles who brings to him the 'plans of Zeus'.[74] At the very end of the play, the hero himself bows his head before the ordinances of the all-powerful God, 'who has brought these things to pass'.[75] There is a strongly religious feeling here, a realization that the ultimate arbiter of human affairs is not men at all but the mysterious designs of the gods. We are not so very far from Romans 'So it comes not from him who wills or runs, but from God who shows mercy'[76] and Augustine's comment: 'It remains for us to recognize that these words are said truly, that all may be given to God, who makes the good will of man ready for his help and helps the will he has made ready'.[77] Again the interface between divine and human is hard to establish.

Euripides, though less influenced by the idea of the ultimate power of the gods, attributes both in his *Bacchae* and *Hippolytus* the downfall of both Pentheus and of Hippolytus to their resistance to forces they should not resist, the powers of wine and love, of Bacchus and Aphrodite. It is easy to treat Euripides simply as a portrayer of an anti-religious rationalism, as in a once popular book *Euripides the Rationalist*.[78] Rather is he aware of the power of the divine to knock people down if they persist in resisting the power of the supernatural world. As the final chorus of the *Bacchae* reminds us: 'The Gods have many shapes and achieve their ends in a way beyond our hopes'.[79] God has in a way become internalized.

The philosophers – Presocratics

When we come to the more philosophic Greeks it seems fair to say that the idea of a supreme reality arose either from reflection on the nature of the universe or of the moral law, and not from

[73]Sophocles, *Oedipus Rex*, verse 1329.
[74]Sophocles, *The Philoctetes*, 1415.
[75]Sophocles, *The Philoctetes*, 1467.
[76]Rom. 9.16.
[77]Augustine, *Handbook*, Section 32 commenting on Rom. 9.16.
[78]W. Verrall, *Euripides the Rationalist*, 2nd edition (Cambridge, 2005).
[79]*Bacchae*, 1388.

history. In their religion, even the names of the gods admit to some connection with the physical universe. Zeus, for example, is the sky god and Hera the goddess of the air. The poets dealt with the traditional myths of the Greeks. The earliest philosophers looked to the natural order for their inspiration.

Aristotle, to whom we are largely indebted for our knowledge of the Presocratic philosophers, states that: 'Most of the earliest philosophers conceived only of material principles as underlying all things'.[80] The Presocratics were fascinated by the problem of change, and approached it by attributing all change and indeed all reality to the dominance of one of four elements or material causes – earth, air with Anaximenes and Diogenes, fire with Heraclitus of Ephesus and water with Thales.

Pythagoras (530 BC) explained all with the idea of numbers as the basis of reality and reduced all ultimately to the idea of a supreme monad.[81] So Aristotle writes: 'The Pythagoreans applied themselves to mathematics and were the first to develop this science'.[82] Finally Parmenides conceived of the absoluteness of the One. 'Everything that is, is one'.[83] There seems to be relatively little religiosity in the speculations of the Presocratics. Even so the idea of the absolute simplicity of the primal monad was to have an important future in Christian as well as Hellenistic thought: Origen calls God a monad[84] and Plotinus insists on the absolute simplicity of the One.[85]

But philosophy itself takes on differing senses with the progress of time, except, that is, in its general sense of a discipline that draws its premises from reason rather than from revelation. The materialistic solutions offered by the Presocratics failed to satisfy later thinkers and in the later fifth century philosophy fell under the influence of the Sophistic movement, which was above all interested in teaching people to speak and argue effectively for any position. This movement, exemplified by men like Gorgias of Leontini, also became interested in facing moral and practical issues and had a less speculative outreach. It made people capable of arguing cleverly

---

[80]Aristotle, *Metaphysics*, book 1, Chapter 3.
[81]Jaap Mansfeld, *Die Vorsokratiker*, 1, (Berlin, 1983) p. 146, no. 30.
[82]Aristotle, *Metaphysics*, Chapter 5.
[83]Plato, *Parmenides*, 143a.
[84]Origen, *On First Principles* book 1, 1: 6.
[85]Plotinus, *Ennead* book 6, 9: 1.

without on the whole offering any firm solution to the more pressing problems of life. There seem to have been so many different ethical codes that relativistic conclusions were the only ones that the great Protagoras was capable of drawing.

The philosophers – Plato

The influence of ethical codes is discernible, for example, in Plato's earlier dialogues, the *Euthyphro*[86] – 'What is the nature of piety?' and the *Laches* – 'What is courage?' and even in book 1 of the *Republic*, with the question 'What is justice?' These dialogues are all essentially heuristic in character and arrive at no definite conclusions. Later on, however this sophistic cleverness changed in what is called Plato's golden period and saw the production of some of his greatest dialogues, above all the *Republic*, the *Symposium* and the *Phaedo* which offer important answers to the ultimate questions they raise about the nature of justice and of the city of the self and the soul and the aim of human life.

Plato's concern with philosophy seems to have been primarily ethical and not in any obvious way to have been provoked by any specifically religious interest. It is misleading to think of him as above all interested in arriving at some sort of mystical vision of ultimate reality. In fact, however, it was aroused less by any speculative interest or by the desire to attain such experience but rather in order to counteract what he perceived as the moral relativism of his day. This arose partly as a result of the defeat of Athens by Sparta and her allies in the Peloponnesian war in 404 BC and the judicial suicide of Socrates in 399. Partly also it was a result of expanding cultural horizons of which the *History* of Herodotus, with its discovery of remarkably differing ways of dealing with the dead, provides a very instructive example. Herodotus reports:

> When Darius was king, he summoned the Greeks who were with him and asked them what price would persuade them to eat their fathers' dead bodies. They answered that there was no price for which they would do it. Then he summoned some black skinned

---

[86][428/7–348/7].

Indians who eat their parents, and asked them in the presence of the Greeks who understood with the aid of an interpreter, what would bring them to burn their fathers at death. The Indians cried out that he should not speak of so horrid an act. So firmly rooted are these beliefs.[87]

Plato endeavoured, as a sort of challenge to this, to establish a more solid basis for the moral order than ancestral custom or mere habit. In his more mature dialogues he does indeed postulate certain ultimate ideas which he located in the intelligible world. This, so the argument ran, was the home of ultimate, unchangeable moral principles: sometimes it was the idea of the good,[88] sometimes that of the beautiful.[89]

The way to perceiving the ultimate was reserved for those and those only who were prepared to subject themselves to a stringent programme of moral and mental preparation. It was not an egalitarian project as Plato himself observes: 'I do not think there will be many philosophers',[90] but the underlying assumption of all these quests is that the world is rationally organized and that questions are there to be both asked and answered. How we are to think of the forms is not altogether clear. As Julia Annas writes: 'If we ask "What are the Forms?" we find a variety of answers . . . a central thought is that the form F is what has the quality F essentially'.[91] Absolute beauty is not something that is beautiful in some ways and not in others. Plato writes: 'The idea of beauty is not, like other things, partly beautiful and partly deformed, not at one time beautiful and at another time not . . . not here beautiful and there deformed . . . but it is essentially uniform and consistent'.[92]

On the whole there is no very clear relationship between cult and philosophy from the fourth century BC with Plato to the second century AD. It is true that the *Republic* begins with the sacrifice to the goddess and the *Phaedo* ends with Socrates' final instructions

---

[87]Herodotus, *History*, book 3, Section 38.
[88]Plato, *Republic* 6.
[89]Plato, *Symposium* 210.
[90]Plato, *Republic* 494a.
[91]J. Annas, 'Classical Greek Philosophy' in *Oxford History of Greece and the Hellenistic World*, J. Boardman, J. Griffin, O. Murray (eds) (Oxford University Press, 1991), p. 289.
[92]Plato, *Symposium* 211a, trans. Shelley.

about sacrificing a cock to Asculapius. But this is never brought into a clear relationship with the search for moral absolutes. Although he expelled the poets from his ideal state because of the unworthy picture they offered of the gods, Plato seems less concerned to provide a revamped pantheon than to create an alternative value system. In the ideal world of forms the supreme reality is essentially impersonal. It would be hard to imagine Plato or anyone else being invited to pray to the Good or worship the One. It is certainly never called Zeus.

A further important aspect of Platonic philosophy, which was to have a lasting effect on later writers of all schools, was his teaching about the nature of the soul. For Plato the soul is a divine spark, which is never really at home in the body. Whether the soul is thought of as simple, as in the *Phaedo* or as tripartite – rational, acquisitive and spirited – as in the *Phaedrus* and the *Republic*, it is always here on probation, before it returns to its proper home in heaven, from which it once fell. For Plato the soul was not simply the principle of sentient life, dwelling in the body and enabling life, growth and sensation. It was also that which in us accounted for our powers of reflection and memory and understanding. By means of these we rise above the purely material, and the world of time and change.

This dualistic view does not necessarily imply a quasi-Gnostic belief in the evil of matter. Even so Plato writes on several occasions as though the main purpose of life was to prepare for death,[93] he also describes the body as a tomb[94] – an idea which is reinforced by a play on words; body in Greek is *soma* and tomb is *sema*.

In later antiquity the dialogue which exercised above all a profound influence upon pagans and Christians alike was Plato's *Timaeus*. It contains several ideas which became fairly standard. The index to the Oxford text of Plotinus devotes six columns to the *Republic* and eight to the *Timaeus*. To begin with, God is there said to be difficult to grasp, 'now to discover the maker and Father of the universe were a task indeed; and having discovered him to declare him unto all men were a thing impossible'.[95] This passage is cited by Origen[96] and is there described by Henry Chadwick

[93] Plato, *Phaedo* 81a.
[94] Plato, *Gorgias* 493a.
[95] Plato, *Timaeus* 28c.
[96] Origen, *Against Celsus* 7:42.

as 'perhaps the most hackneyed of all quotations from Plato in Hellenistic writers'.[97]

A little further on, the answer to the question, 'Why did God create the universe?' is stated to be his goodness and the absence in him of any envy – a view endorsed by a whole host of writers, pagan[98] and Christian alike. Finally, in the account of the making of the world the *Timaeus* adduces three primary principles – the ideal pattern of the universe to be found in the world of forms; the demiurge or designer, who acts with his mind's eye on the forms; and finally the pre-existent matter, which Plato calls 'the nurse of becoming'.[99]

We are therefore required to imagine a God, who though personal and deeply mysterious, is still less absolute than the impersonal world of forms he contemplates. He then, like a master craftsman, fashions the matter that lies before him into varied shapes. As later Christian writers were quick to point out, valuable though this picture of reality might be, it fell short of later orthodoxy on two counts. It made God inferior to the absolute world of reality and it also made God dependent upon the material at his disposal. The God of the *Timaeus* is no creator God, in the sense to be later discussed – of making something out of nothing. He is more like a poet, organizing the material elements at his disposal in order to create a beautiful artefact.

The philosophers – Aristotle

Aristotle's (384–322 BC) approach is, if possible, even less religious and certainly more this worldly in its emphasis. This aspect of Aristotle is illustrated by the perhaps malicious story that he recanted (or played safe) at the end of his life by stipulating in his will[100] the erection in Stagira, after his death, of two statues to Zeus and Athena 'the saviours' – a strange expression for Aristotle.

---

[97]H. Chadwick, in Origen, *Against Celsus*, trans. H. Chadwick, p. 429.
[98]Athanasius expressly refers to it in Chapter 3 of *On the Incarnation*.
[99]Plato, *Timaeus* 52d.
[100]This we learn from his will preserved for us by Diogenes Laertius in his third century (AD) *Lives of the Philosophers* [5;1,16].

At the beginning of his *Nicomachean Ethics*, Aristotle makes it clear that he is distinguishing his own position from that of his master, Plato, by rejecting both the theory of forms and the notion of the separateness and immortality of the soul, the two distinctive features of traditional Platonism. Aristotle realizes that he is consciously distinguishing his position from that of Plato with the observation 'Friends and truth are both dear, but truth is more important'.[101] For him the good is an idea realized in a number of particular instances. The definition is what is had in common, and is not a supra terrestrial reality.

Likewise the soul is not a temporary visitor from outer space; rather it is the form of the body separated from which it has no independent existence. In book 2 of Aristotle's treatise *On the Soul*, he distinguishes in a general way between the matter of which things are made and the form that gives them shape. So, for example, a table is a composite made of wood and the shape the wood bears. He then applies this to the human being. 'The soul must be substance in the sense of being the form of a natural body, which potentially has life. The soul, then, is the actuality of the kind of body we have described . . . it is a substance expressed as a form'.[102] If the soul's essential role is to be the form of the body and to be the source of sensation, nutrition, thought and motion, it follows that it is inappropriate to think of it as somehow detachable from that of which it is the life principle. Plato's vision of the soul as a prisoner from another world is a long way off. Immortality, Aristotle elsewhere writes is beyond our reach.[103]

The source of order in the universe was to be found in the idea of the supreme mover, a being conceived as a final rather than efficient or material cause, drawing all things by desire. Aristotle writes: 'the object of desire and the object of thought move without being moved'.[104] This prime mover was thought of as quite distinct from the traditional gods. It is further defined as 'self thinking thought',[105] thought being the most noble activity to which any reality can aspire. 'For the actuality of thought is life and God is

---

[101] Aristotle, *Ethics* I, VI:4.
[102] Aristotle, *On the Soul*, 412a.
[103] Aristotle, *Ethics* 3, 2:4.
[104] Aristotle, *Metaphysics* 12, Chapter 7.
[105] Aristotle, *Metaphysics*, 99, 1074, 8–14.

that actuality; and the essential actuality of God is life most good and eternal'.[106] We have travelled a long way from the traditional gods of the Greek pantheon, but the similarity between Aristotle's God and that of reflective Christianity is patent.

Despite the fact that Plato and to a lesser extent Aristotle had a practical aim, it is even so true that the main thrust of their writings was primarily intellectual in intention. In both writers the aim of the moral life is the preparation of the person for the understanding of the truth. Plato thought, as we have seen, that the ideal philosopher must be prepared to lead a moral even an ascetic existence, and further than that, to be ready to descend from his contemplation of absolute reality to attend to the needs of the prisoners in the cave. Aristotle devoted the first nine books of his *Nicomachean Ethics* to moral virtue. The tenth and final book is devoted to contemplation, which is not only the highest human activity but also one which introduces the serious and moral thinker into the divine world, 'where we shall become divine through contemplation'.[107] This connexion is facilitated by a word play. The Greek word for god is '*theos*' and that for contemplate is '*theorein*'.

The philosophers – Stoicism

The word Stoic and its derivative Stoicism have their root in the Greek word Stoa or porch, where the founders of the school, Zeno (335–263 BC), Cleanthes (331–323 BC) and Chrysippus (280–207 BC) delivered their lectures. Unlike Plato and Aristotle, their primary interest was intensely practical. Its foundation coincided roughly with the deaths of Demosthenes and Aristotle in 322 BC and with the death of the city state for which the great orator Demosthenes had delivered his Philippics in his unsuccessful attempt to halt the advance of Philip of Macedon on Athens. The defeat of Athens and the subsequent rise of the worldwide empire of Philip's son, Alexander the Great (355–323 BC), put an end to the idea of a city state not only of Athens but also elsewhere.

The popularity of Stoicism was in large measure due to the simple fact that it enabled people to live modest and useful lives within a

---

[106]Aristotle, *Metaphysics* 12: 7,9.
[107]Aristotle, *Ethics* 10: 7.

world empire, over which the ordinary private person had little or no hope of exercising any significant influence. It amounted in practice to the useful advice to restrict your aims and objectives within the realm of the practicable, and this ethical doctrine gave great comfort to many during the troubled times that followed the 'death' of Athens as an independent city, no longer able to decide its own destiny.

Unlike both Plato and Aristotle, the early Stoics seem to have had no belief in the existence of a transcendent reality, personal or otherwise. But despite this apparently atheistic stance, in which God was little more than the soul of the world, it is perhaps surprising to find Cleanthes addressing a *Hymn to Zeus*, which opens with the following invocation: 'Hail, O Zeus, most glorious of the immortals, named by many names, forever all powerful, leader of nature . . . O Zeus, giver of all, shrouded in dark clouds, master of the bright thunderbolt, save men from painful ignorance'.[108] We are a long way from academic Stoicism, which serves to underline the point that even philosophy may be inconsistent, just as Plato and Aristotle continued their religious practices despite their philosophical opinions.

Stoicism under the empire

At the period when Christianity was born, the philosophical horizon was largely dominated by a form of eclectic Stoicism and not by a modified form of Plato – neither middle nor later Platonism, for reasons that are not entirely clear, succeeded in reasserting itself as the dominant philosophy of the empire until the second half of the second century AD. It may be that during that period, Platonism was only slowly emancipating itself from the clutches of the scepticism into which it had relapsed above all under Carneades, the leader of the New Academy. It has also been suggested that with the increased insistence in the second century AD on style in education, Plato's popularity may owe something to the elegant lucidity of his Greek.

It is a truism that whereas ordinary people sought to deepen their lives by means of the cults discussed in the following, the more sophisticated sought relief in the earlier imperial epoch in Stoicism. Seneca (4 BC–65 AD), the unlucky tutor of the emperor Nero forced

---

[108] J. U. Powell (ed.), *Collectanea Alexandrina*.

by his pupil to commit suicide, is less consistently Stoic in his outlook offering a view of the world which adopts ideas that seem more at home in Platonism. Epictetus (55–135 AD) the Stoic sage and former slave and Marcus Aurelius, emperor from 161–180, whose *Meditations* were composed while on campaign in Hungary continue this tradition. Even so it is true that the primary thrust of imperial Stoicism was aimed at helping people to be at home in an at times hostile world, by self knowledge and an awareness of the limits placed upon them by both their own abilities and by the society they lived in.

All three writers are somewhat eclectic in their approach. They incorporated elements of which writers like Zeno and Chrysippus would have probably disapproved. They were happy on occasion to use language about the universe that implied a belief in a personal being or god. Even so, despite what might be called the revisionary character of imperial Stoicism, it is hard to disagree with Fernand Braudel, who states that despite Seneca and Marcus Aurelius the Romans 'simply plagiarised their [Greek] predecessors'.[109]

Seneca's philosophy emerges most clearly in a series of letters, which in effect amount to treatises written to his friend Lucilius. The amazing similarity that some of his sentences bear to the letters of Saint Paul suggests that even though they were unlikely to have been aware of each others writings, they breathed a similar atmosphere. For example, letter 42 opens with a statement that reminds one of 1 Cor. 3.16. Seneca writes: 'God is near you, he is with you, he is within you . . . a holy spirit [sacer spiritus] dwells within us', Saint Paul writes: 'Do you not know that you are God's temple and that God's spirit dwells within you'. Again the thought of the church as a living body[110] is not far away from the idea of the universe as a body enlivened by the presence in it of its soul, which is God.[111] Saint Paul writes as follows: 'For just as the body is one and has many members and all the members of the body, though many are one body, so it is with Christ'.[112] Seneca writes as follows: 'That which creates, in other words God, is more powerful and precious than matter, which is acted upon by God. God's place in

---

[109] F. Braudel, *The Mediterranean in the Ancient World*, (Allen Lane, 2001), p. 343.
[110] 1 Cor. 12.12 ff.
[111] Seneca, *Epistles*, 3 vols, trans. R. M. Gummere, (Loeb Classical Library, Harvard University Press, 1917, 1920, 1925), 65, 24.
[112] 1 Cor. 12.12.

the universe corresponds to the soul's relation to man. World matter corresponds to our mortal body'.[113]

Again, although Stoics in theory denied the existence of a transcendent, otherworldly deity, in practice they use theistic language, as we have seen was the case with Cleanthes. Seneca, for example, despite his belief in the universal presence of the divine in nature can also attribute to him powers of creation, writes: 'God has created all the great number of leaves that we behold, each stamped with its special pattern'.[114]

The practical nature of the Stoic approach is well illustrated by a sentence in Epictetus – the second of the three writers mentioned earlier. He was himself a freed slave, who had learnt how to preserve a free spirit despite the constraints of his existence. He writes:

Men, the lecture room of the philosopher is a hospital; you ought not to walk out of it in pleasure but in pain. For you are not well when you come. Then am I to sit down and write to you dainty little notions and clever little mottoes, so that you will depart with words of praise on your lips, one man carrying away his shoulder just as it was when he came in.[115]

In other words we should go to philosophy, not in a speculative spirit, but in one which seeks rather a remedy from moral sickness.

Epictetus also sums up his somewhat submissive philosophy with the epigram 'Bear and forebear'. Acceptance of what cannot be avoided whether in oneself or in one's companions or in society at large may be a good recipe for peace of soul, but it is hardly likely to change the existing situation, however unsatisfactory or vicious that might be. Changing the world is clearly not part of the agenda of Epictetus. This connects up with Epictetus' attitude to evil. Possessions or absence of them are neither good nor evil. We naturally as human beings fell from evil and pursue good. 'But it is not the externals that are good or evil, there is only one thing that is truly good, the right kind of moral purpose . . . and that alone is bad, which is the wrong kind of moral purpose'.[116]

---

[113]Seneca, *Epistles*, 92, 30.
[114]Seneca, *Epistles*, 113, 16.
[115]Epictetus, *Discourses*, book III, xxiii: 30.
[116]Epictetus, *Discourses*, book iv, 5:33.

Epictetus, likewise, on several occasions refers to a mysterious 'Other' by which he presumably means God. He writes: 'This is your business, to play admirably the role assigned to you; but the selection of that role is Another's'.[117] He does this despite the fact that for the Stoics, God is the soul of the world, a thoroughly immanentist idea. He opens Chapter 31 of the *Enchiridion* with the following statement: 'In piety towards the Gods, I would have you know that the chief element is this, to have correct opinions about them and to have set yourself to obey them'. Most surprising of all is a celebrated passage where he writes about the formula 'Lord, have mercy'.[118] God, he argues, knows what is best for you therefore we should not try to corrupt his judgement by that sort of prayer. Is this a covert attack on Christian practice? Very possibly, or the similarity may only be accidental. But if the latter alternative is preferable, it points undoubtedly to a similarity of religious feeling, if not of actual belief at this period.

Marcus Aurelius' explanation of the great difficulty facing any believer either in the divine goodness and omnipotence or in a benign overarching providence is the problem of evil. His solution to the problem differs from that of Epictetus. Epictetus, as we have seen, locates evil not in some physical event, but in the habit of mind we bring to our circumstances. Marcus, however, asks the very practical question: 'How are we to explain the existence in the world of the bitter gherkin and of briars in the path?'.[119] The answer offered is that they are a necessary part of the universal process. 'The marvel of her craftsmanship is that though she is limited to herself, she transmuted into her own substance, all that within her seems perishing and decrepit and useless'. In other words the overarching providence is able to make use of what we might be inclined to dismiss as useless.

The severely practical nature of philosophy also emerges when asked 'What then is it that can help us on our way? One thing and one thing alone – Philosophy; and this consists in keeping the divine genius within us pure'.[120] Marcus Aurelius can write of a world full of

---

[117]Epictetus, *Enchiridion*, 17.
[118]Epictetus, *Discourses*, book ii, 7.
[119]Marcus Aurelius, *Meditations*, trans. C. R. Haines, (Loeb Classical Library, Harvard University Press, 1916), book viii, 50.
[120] Marcus Aurelius, *Meditations*, book ii, 17.

gods by which he means the divine providence and the nature of the whole. 'If there are no gods, or if they do not concern themselves with the affairs of men, why should I live in a world empty of gods or empty of providence? But there are gods and they do concern themselves with human things'.[121] Here we find Marcus pretty well identifying providence with God. This was clearly a thought that sustained him in his demanding duties. When all allowances have been made it must be stated that there is something inexpressibly noble in the way Marcus faces the challenges he meets daily, as emperor. Strangely, after so powerful an advocate, Stoicism found no worthy successor.

Roman religion and the mystery cults

Nothing has so far been said about the official religion of Rome, which concentrated upon the formal worship of the old twelve gods of the Greek pantheon, to which was added in the imperial period, the cult of the genius of the Roman Emperor. Far from implying a commitment to the values or even to the existence of gods like Jupiter and Juno, one of the principal reasons for the existence and cult of these beings lay in the social and political cohesion that any established religion provides. Indeed it was for their failure to conform on this very issue that made the Christians of the imperial period deeply suspect and subsequently persecuted. Much of the writing of the second century writers of defences of Christianity is devoted to dealing with the Christian refusal to join in common worship.

Yet despite its social usefulness it cannot be said that the official religion of Rome satisfied the deeper spiritual aspirations of many ordinary people. The deficit was supplied by the emergence not only of philosophy, above all Stoic philosophy in the early empire, but also of the so-called mystery religions, which offered by means of a sacred and usually hidden rite to establish contact with the objects of their worship. The cults of Mithra (for soldiers), Isis (for women) and of Dionysus at Eleusis promised secret knowledge and above all experience that the official cults were quite unable to supply.

Though originating as a light god in Iran and India, the cult of Mithra spread to the Roman Empire and became established at the

---

[121]Marcus Aurelius, *Meditations*, book ii, 11.

end of the first century AD. The rites, for men only, were celebrated in underground temples dominated by the representation of the slaying of a bull by the light god, Mithra. The rite culminated in a sacred meal. The system contained the notion of the ascent of the soul through seven stages till its arrival in heaven. The third century Christian writer, Origen, cites a passage from his pagan adversary, Celsus, which describes this ascent.

The evident similarities between Christian worship and the mysteries of Mithra, especially the ideas of the victory of light and the sacred meal suggested to some critics of the gospel, then and now, that the Christians had borrowed their secret ceremonies from the votaries of Mithra. This claim was vigorously rejected by Justin Martyr.[122] After providing an account of the Eucharist, Justin carries on to the effect that the wicked demons imitated the Christian rites by introducing bread and water to their own ceremonies 'with some words said over them'.

The earliest account we possess of the Eleusinian mysteries in honour of the god Dionysius also occurs in a Christian writer, Clement of Alexandria, who says 'the mysteries of Dionysus are of a perfectly savage character'[123]. Clement then proceeds to describe the mythical youth of the god and his destruction by the Titans. The limbs of Dionysus were subsequently entrusted for burial by Zeus to Apollo. The actual mysteries purported to re-enact the strange history of the god. It is important to note that the mysteries made great moral demands upon their votaries and in some way brought them fuller life through their participation in the actual rite. There are evident similarities here to the Christian Eucharist and Clement's attack more than suggests that they were perceived as serious rivals to Christianity. Both shared the conviction that communion with God demanded moral virtue and was the doorway to a life of rebirth through eating the body of God.

Later Platonic philosophy

Despite the fact that in the first century BC Platonists, like Philo of Larisa and Antiochus of Askalon, attempted to rescue Platonism

---

[122] Justin Martyr, *First Apology*, Chapter 66.
[123] Clement of Alexandria, *Exhortation to the Greeks*, Chapter 2.

from its negatively critical standpoint, for reasons that are not altogether clear they failed to dislodge Stoicism from its privileged position as the leading philosophy of the day till the middle and latter part of the second century. The fact is that no Stoic writer of any distinction appears after the end of the second century AD, that is, after Marcus Aurelius. It may be that the revival of interest in Plato arose under the influence of the Second Sophistic movement largely as a result of stylistic criteria.

The first and second centuries AD witnessed a coming together of the Platonic and Aristotelian traditions in what is called Middle Platonism, a philosophy exemplified in writers like Plutarch and Alcinous. Plutarch (c. 46AD to c. 120AD) came from Boeotia and was a priest at the shrine of Apollo at Delphi. His interest in religious issues expressed itself in some of his treatises, the *Moralia*. His treatise on the Egyptian deities Isis and Osiris, begins with a plea for truth. In his writings there appears no divorce, as there does in those of Plato, between religion and philosophy. One of his treatises, *On the E at Delphi*, offers an explanation of the letter E, which appeared there together with two other sayings of the Delphic oracle: 'Know thyself' and 'Nothing in excess'. In Section 17 of the treatise a solution to the meaning of 'E' is proposed by Ammonius, who argues that it means 'Thou art' and that it assigns to Apollo alone true and absolute being. Hardly surprisingly the ecclesiastical historian Eusebius quotes this passage with approval,[124] coinciding as it does with the self definition of God offered to Moses: 'I am who I am'.[125]

Of Alcinous or Albinus very little is known, except that he taught the physician, Galen and therefore lived in the middle of the second century AD. For him the ultimate or primal being, which or rather whom he describes in Chapter 10 of his *Handbook*, is always called god and is also both ineffable and graspable only by the intellect – an echo of Plato's *Timaeus* 28c. For the *Handbook*, as we shall see later in Chapter 3, god is both demiurge and eternal. Moreover whereas Plato and Aristotle had made a separation between religion and philosophy, this dichotomy was in large measure overcome in the imperial era, as had the traditional distinction between Plato and Aristotle.

---

[124]Eusebius, *Preparation for the Gospel*, book xii.
[125]Exod. 3.14.

With a view to comparing a little later the theology of Origen with that of the Middle Platonism of Alcinous (c 150 AD), Apuleius and Numenius, it will be helpful to provide an outline of their respective systems, above all of their strictly so called theologies. In doing this it is important to remember that some writers in the Platonic school, notably Plutarch and Atticus, rejected the tendency to forge an amalgam, Alcinous (or Albinus) was enough of a Platonist to postulate in his *Handbook* three basic principles after the manner of the *Timaeus*:[126] matter, that is 'the mould' or the 'nurse of becoming' in Chapter 8 – all terms taken from that dialogue; the forms or the paradigmatic cause in Chapter 9; and God the efficient cause in Chapter 10.

Alcinous outlines the central characteristics of the primal god as follows: he is 'superior to soul, superior to potential intellect and superior to actual intellect'.[127] Again he is 'eternal, ineffable, self perfect . . . He is the Good . . . the Beautiful'. We can learn something of this mysterious being by abstraction, by analogy and by ascent. Alcinous' language here is strikingly close to that of Celsus, as recorded by Origen.[128] The third way is outlined after the manner of the ascent to Beauty in Plato's *Symposium*.[129] We can see even in this brief outline how Alcinous combines in his idea of the primal god, elements that properly belong both to Plato, above all the *Republic* and the *Symposium*, goodness and beauty and to Aristotle, in his *Metaphysics* L with its account of self thinking thought.

In addition to the god in repose, the primary god, Alcinous seems also to postulate a secondary being that is in motion and directed downwards. The primary is simple, the secondary is complex. This second god has close affinities with the *Logos* of Philo, who acts as an intermediate entity between the transcendent, first God and the world of time and change. A similar picture emerges from the surviving fragments of Numenius, a Pythagorean philosopher from Apamea in Syria, who retried to effect a fusion between the thought of Plato and that of Moses. He was probably a contemporary of Marcus Aurelius. Numenius is cited by name

---

[126] *Timaeus*, 27a5–6.
[127] Alcinous [aka Alibnus] *Handbook* 10, 2 note 130 10.3.
[128] Origen, *Against Celsus* 7,42.
[129] *Symposium* 210 ff.

by Origen on several occasions with approval: 'I am also aware
that Numenius the Pythagorean, a man who expounded Plato with
very great skill, and maintained the Pythagorean doctrines, quotes
Moses and the prophets in many of his writings, giving them an
allegorical explanation'.[130] He used language with which to denote
the second god of his system that closely parallels that of Origen.
In fragments 11, 15 and 16 of his treatise *On the Good*, he seems
to have distinguished three levels of being all called gods and
each of increasing complexity. This pattern of declension became
increasingly popular in the second century AD among Christians
like Origen and Neoplatonists like Plotinus.

Alcinous' clear identification of the more personal God of
Aristotle with the impersonal absolute of Plato was important
for Christians, even though not all Platonists accepted it. This is
important above all because it helps to answer the difficulty of
German classical scholars like Heinrich Doerries.[131] He insists on
a radical difference between Christian theology and Hellenism. His
metaphor with which to describe the relationship between the two
is that of the hermit crab. In other words certain surface external
appearances of similarity hide profound differences. One of his
arguments runs as follows: Plato's account of creation subordinates
the personal demiurge to the impersonal forms, God does geometry
and is above all a master craftsman dependent on both the forms
and on pre-existent matter. Christianity by contrast replaces the
impersonal absolute of Plato with a personal God.

While it is indeed true that third and fourth century Christians
rejected some of Plato's cosmic vision, it needs to be remembered
that despite the nominal adhesion of later Platonism to the master,
much of his teaching had been revised. By the time the second
century AD had arrived a rather different landscape appeared. The
adoption by writers like Alcinous of certain of Aristotle's ideas into
a basically Platonic cadre enabled them to make precisely the fusion
of personal and absolute, which we find in certain second and third
century Christian writers.

---

[130]Origen, *Against Celsus*, 4, 51.
[131]Doerries, H., Gregory von Nyssa und die philosophie, Brill 1976.

Plotinus (205–270)

This process of assimilation and amalgamation characterizes later Platonism, with one significant exception – Plotinus. He always thought of himself as essentially a commentator on Plato in much the same way as Christian writers treated Saint Paul as 'the divine apostle' and as earlier writers had treated Homer. Plotinus returned to a more strictly Platonic perspective and elevated the absolute above Mind and personality. He termed it the One or the Good, but only very occasionally god. But the idea of praying to someone beyond being finds no place in the *Enneads*. Plotinus, unlike both his immediate predecessors and his followers, is recorded to have had no interest whatever in religion, even in the limited sense of Plato, whose philosophy and religion were kept in separate compartments, as the opening of the *Republic* and the end of the *Phaedo* illustrate.

His biographer Porphyry relates that on one occasion Plotinus was invited to attend temple worship and he gave the somewhat chilling reply: 'It is they that should come to me not I to them'.[132] However, it is probably true to say that Plotinus' lack of interest in formal religion was not typical of the Platonic school of the period. Neither Porphyry nor Iamblichus (who died in about 326 AD) followed him in this. The latter's treatise *De Mysteriis* (*On the Mysteries*) is a deliberate refutation of the attempt made by Porphyry to devalue mystery religion. It is odd to think that Plotinus was untypical of the school of which he was the greatest ornament.

Beneath the One, but derived from it in a way that is not altogether clear, comes the second hypostasis or Mind as he calls it. And beneath Mind is the third principle or World Soul. Beneath the World Soul is matter, or where the light fades out. Evil and matter are essentially negative. They are where the light (and therefore being) fades out. The essentially negative character of evil was later to be found of great use in their theodicy by Gregory of Nyssa in the East and Augustine in the West. But even with Plotinus, we are reminded of Marcus Aurelius' doctrine that the power of the One is so great that it can make use of what is evil. So he can write: 'Not

---

[132]Porphyry, *Life of Plotinus*, trans. A. H. Armstrong, (Loeb Classical Library, Harvard University Press, 1969), Chapter 10.

that evil exists for this purpose; but as we have indicated, once the wrong has come to be, the Reason of the Cosmos employs it to good ends'.[133] Such an approach seems to assign a more positive character to evil than the negative approach of *Ennead* i, 8. Such an attitude to the problem of evil was adopted frequently by Augustine, who argues that God displays his almighty power above all in his ability to draw good out of evil. He writes: 'God did not deprive man of his free will, because he at the same time foresaw what good he himself would bring out of evil'.[134]

For Plotinus there are no straight lines across the map of the universe. The three hypostases, the One, Mind and Soul are linked together, though distinct. It is not altogether clear how Plotinus reconciled the continuity and discontinuity of reality. The former idea means that we who belong to the realm of the World Soul are always somehow in touch with the higher world of Mind; the latter suggests a distinction among the three principal hypostases. It may be that this very ambiguity recommended itself to later Christian theologians as they wrestled with the mystery of the unity and trinity of God.

In any event, we can make this conviction more real by asceticism and contemplation, in some instances rising to ecstasy. Plotinus himself, it would seem, had his own moments of ecstasy on four occasions, though he never refers to them himself. These spiritual experiences probably made him less aware of the need for traditional religion. Porphyry writes: 'to Plotinus at any rate, the goal was ever near, for his end and goal was to be united with and close to the god above all. This goal he achieved four times, while I was with him, not virtually but in unspeakable actuality'.[135]

Even so the particular genius of Plotinus was too rarefied for the foundation of a school. Writers like Porphyry and even more so Iamblichus were more traditional in their desire to be religious as well as philosophical. This fusion of the two was no doubt encouraged by the growing confidence of Christianity, with its effort in writers like Justin to separate classical philosophy from polytheism and unite the philosophical side of Hellenism to

---

[133]Plotinus, *Enneads*, 7 vols, trans. A. H. Armstrong, (Loeb Classical Library, Harvard University Press, 1969, 1966, 1967, 1984, 1984, 1988, 1988), *Ennead* iii, 2, 5
[134]Augustine, *City of God*, book 22, Chapter 1.
[135]Porphyry, *The Life of Plotinus*, Chapter 23.

the Christian gospel. Pagans like Celsus had reacted against this assumption and in his *True Account*, written probably in about 173 AD, began to insist on the integrity of Hellenism and reject the divorce between Greek religion and philosophy proposed by Justin, and to some extent endorsed by Plotinus. In this move to defend the integrity of classical culture, Celsus was followed by Porphyry and Julian. Part of Augustine's aim of the *City of God* above all in book 10 was to show the Pagans they did not have a monopoly, either of learning or philosophy and most of his references are to Porphyry.

Plotinus occurs by name in the earlier account of his conversion and even there, there is a textual variant. We read 'Plato's visage, which is the most pure and bright in philosophy, shone forth once the clouds of error had been dispelled, and above all in Plotinus'.[136] He is also referred to twice again in the *City of God*, on both occasions as a commentator on Plato. Augustine writes 'Plotinus enjoys the reputation of having understood Plato better than any other of his disciples'.[137] Finally he attributes the doctrine of intelligible illumination to Plotinus.[138] For Augustine, Plotinus was above all the archetypal Platonist, and it was as such that Plotinus regarded himself. Quotations above all from the *Phaedrus*, the *Republic* and *Timaeus* of the divine philosopher are very frequent.

Porphyry (232/233–303)

Of all the disciples of Plotinus, Porphyry was without a doubt the most influential and certainly the most prolific. He came from Tyre and it is to him that we owe our knowledge of Plotinus' life and the collection and organization of his *Enneads*. The appendix to a recent translation of his *Launching Points to the Realm of Mind*, an introduction to the philosophy of his master Plotinus in 44 chapters, lists no less than 77 works and many of these titles represent a medley of writings. Most of his writings have perished, including 200 books *On Matter* and 15 *Against the Christians*. As has already been mentioned, Augustine refers to him frequently and it may be that to Porphyry rather than to Plotinus that he owed his knowledge

---

[136]In Section 4 of his *On the Blessed Life*, In *Against the Academics* 3.41.
[137]Augustine, *City of God*, 9: 10.
[138]Augustine, *City of God*,10: 2.

of Neoplatonism. Unlike his master, he was overtly hostile to Christianity, and it was in order to give intellectual respectability to the renewed outbreak of persecution under Diocletian in 302 that Porphyry composed his treatise *Against the Christians*, most of which was destroyed by order of the emperor Theodosius 2 in 448.

Porphyry's attitude to religious practices differed from that of his master, as did his attempt to unite the ideas of unity and threefoldness in the spiritual world. He was prepared to give some sort of acceptance to theurgy, which is the belief that our souls and our bodies can be aided in their upward ascent by the use of external religious exercises. So Augustine writes of him: 'Even Porphyry promises some sort of purgation of the soul by the help of theurgy, though he does so with some hesitation and shame, and denies that this art can secure to any one a return to God'.[139] The tension between religion and philosophy is evident from this brief extract.

The fact that Augustine selected Porphyry as the prime target for his attack on philosophical paganism may indicate an awareness that he posed more of a threat to the gospel than did the more cerebral Plotinus It was to him that he was in all probability indebted for his intellectual conversion as related in book 7 of the *Confessions*, though there Porphyry is not mentioned by name, any more than is Plotinus whose name is only rarely recorded by Augustine. In the *Confessions* at any rate he prefers the vaguer expression 'books of the Platonists'. On three occasions[140] Augustine refers to the 'books of the Platonists' as translated by Marius Victorinus, but without being more specific.

---

[139] Augustine, *City of God*, book x, Chapter 9.
[140] Augustine, *Confessions*, twice in book 7 and once in book 6.

2

Saint Paul, the Apostolic Fathers and the Apologists of the second century

Saint Paul and philosophy

In trying to come to terms with Saint Paul's thought, and above all his attitude to philosophy, we need to take seriously the words of E. P. Sanders where he writes on the dangers of treating him as a systematic theologian.[1] His thought was moulded by the differing situations that he was called on to deal with. Some of his converts saw the gospel as an excuse for being libertines[2] and following it as being hardly different from legalism and Judaism.[3] Clearly some of them thought their own secular wisdom was enough, others wished to dispense with it altogether.

Paul was above all a missionary on fire with zeal for his Christ-given faith. His attitude to philosophy has more in common with that of the professional rhetorician, capable of using arguments drawn from philosophy without committing himself to any one system. And what is true of Pauline eclecticism is also true of the Apologists who came after him. In other words they were open to

---

[1] E. P. Sanders, *Paul: A Very Short Introduction*, (Oxford University Press, 2001), p. 149.
[2] As at Romans 6.
[3] As in the celebrated confrontation of Peter and Paul narrated in Galatians 2.

the intelligent world around them, capable of relating to it but not committed to any one expression. In this they shared something with the philosophy that surrounded them.

As we have already seen, even by the middle of the first century BC, previously unheard of amalgams were to be found that united the insights of Plato, Aristotle and the Stoics without apparently being aware that the founders of the various schools and systems would have greeted such eclecticism with some suspicion. For example, how could a true Stoic express belief or appear to express belief in a personal deity, as we have seen Epictetus doing? In other word, eclecticism was not a peculiarity of the Christian apologist.

Unfortunately we know little about the intellectual background and development of Paul. We are forced to depend on the evidence provided by Acts, in itself a questionable procedure, and that offered by his own letters to form some sort of estimate of his knowledge and use of the current philosophy of his day. We do not know what influence Tarsus and Gamaliel exercised upon him. To begin with we find several scattered references to classical poetry.[4] In the second case Paul is offering his second account of his conversion, this time for the benefit of King Agrippa. In it he adds to the words he heard on the way to Damascus, 'Saul, Saul, why are you persecuting me?', the words 'it is hard for you to kick against the pricks'.[5] There are also two passages from his letters 'Evil communications corrupt good manners' from the *Thais* of the Greek comic poet, Menander.[6] Finally in the doubtfully Pauline *Titus* there is a passage about lying Cretans from a work *On Oracles* by Epimenides.[7] All this need only mean that Paul had some acquaintance with handbooks or anthologies without any profound knowledge of the pagan poetry of his day.

Small though this may be, it is more than can be said of any other books of the New Testament, with the solitary exception of Acts, and even there the classical allusions are almost invariably connected with Saint Paul. However seriously we interpret these texts, it is worth noting that no other New Testament subject has

---

[4] Acts 17.28 and Acts 26.14.
[5] Usually taken to be a quotation for the benefit of the king of a passage from the *Bacchae of Euripides*, line 794.
[6] 1 Cor. 15.33.
[7] *Letter to Titus*, 1:12.

any classical quotations attributed to him. This rather suggests that Paul was more in touch with the surrounding culture than were the others.

In the Acts, on one celebrated occasion he borrows language and ideas that belong within a philosophical framework, which is largely Stoic. There, unlike his letters, his usage is neither purely literary nor ornamental. This is above all true of the address delivered on the Areopagus to the Athenian wise men.[8] Paul's address to the learned begins where they are, above all with the mysterious altar to the Unknown God,[9] then by means of a quotation from Aratus, a Stoic poet (315–240 BC),[10] he leads them on to a Stoic conception of the universe, in which each of us belongs to the divine family. The whole passage runs as follows:

> We should seek after God in the hope that they might feel after him and find him. Yet he is not far from each one of us, for "in him we live and move and have our being"; as even one of your poets have said, "For we are indeed his offspring".

However, having carried his audience with him so far, his mention of the resurrection from the dead divided his hearers and shortly afterwards he left Athens for Corinth.

Saint Paul's eloquent and familiar rejection of the value of the philosophy of this world, which occurs above all in the first two chapters of his *First Letter to the Corinthians*, must be seen against this background. These two chapters have become a basic source for those who regard all philosophy as essentially incompatible with the Christian gospel. There we read: 'Has not God made foolish the wisdom of the world?'[11] and 'Yet among the mature we do impart wisdom, although it is not the wisdom of this age or of the rulers of this age, who are doomed to pass away'.[12] In the same letter, he writes: 'Knowledge [gnosis] puffs up, but love builds up'.[13] And elsewhere he warns his converts: 'See that no one makes a prey of you by

---

[8] Acts 17.22 ff.
[9] Acts 17.23.
[10] Acts 17.28.
[11] 1 Cor. 1.20.
[12] 1 Cor. 2.6.
[13] 1 Cor. at the beginning of ch. 8.

philosophy and empty deceit'.[14] Texts like these are sufficiently well known and have given rise to the partially misleading impression that Paul had no use or time for secular thought.

Taken by themselves these Corinthian passages, popular above all with those who wish to sterilize the gospel of alien influences, do not do justice to the full range of 'the divine apostle's' thought on the subject of the place of philosophy in Christianity. As we shall see, Paul is less monolithic than might first appear from this somewhat selective reading. Passages above all in Acts, in his *Letter to the Romans* and even in 1 Corinthians itself serve to dispel too monochrome an understanding of his general stance and so help to modify this impression.

As a counterpoise to the message of 1 Corinthians, the significance of two passages in the first two chapters of his *Letter to the Romans*, where philosophy is employed to support his position, should not be overlooked. There he borrows arguments from the Stoics in order to establish a proof for the existence of God from design.[15] He writes: 'Ever since the creation of the world, his invisible nature, namely his eternal power and deity, has been clearly perceived in men who were ignorant of God and were foolish by nature; and they were unable from the good things that are seen to know him who exists'.[16]

Seneca, who like Paul was condemned to death by Nero, his former pupil, was a near contemporary of Saint Paul. He writes in his *Letter 65* of the 'master builder of the universe', asking: 'Do you forbid me to contemplate the universe? May I not ask what are the beginnings of all things, who moulded the universe? May I not inquire who is the master builder of the universe?'.[17] This is not to suggest that Paul and Seneca had actually met, despite the charming story to that effect, or that Paul, a Greek speaking Jew, knew Latin, but rather to argue that the worlds in which the two writers moved were not totally remote from each other.

Further, when he refers to a 'natural law written on the hearts of men',[18] he is not innovating. The idea of conscience or of an

---

[14]Col. 2.8.
[15]Rom. 1.19-21.
[16]Rom. 1.20.
[17]Seneca, *Epistles*, 65, section 19.
[18]Rom. 2.15.

inner law written on human hearts appears in the Wisdom of Solomon: 'For wickedness is a cowardly thing, condemned by its own testimony; distressed by conscience, it has always exaggerated the difficulties'.[19] Acting in harmony with nature is an ideal held up by all the Stoic philosophers. Seneca writing towards the end of his life in about 63 AD defines the ideal life as one in accordance with nature.[20] In *Letter 54*, he writes:

> The first thing that philosophy undertakes to give is fellow feeling with all men; in other words sympathy and sociability. We part company with our promise if we are unlike other men. Our motto, as you know, is "Live according to nature". But it is quite contrary to nature to torture the body.[21]

Epictetus does so when he writes: 'We must cultivate and perfect our moral purpose to make it harmonious with nature'.[22] Marcus Aurelius likewise speaks of the ideal of a 'life lived in accordance with nature'.[23] The closing sentence of book 2 of the same work reads as follows: 'For it is in the way of nature, and in the way of nature there can be no evil'.

One further instance of Paul's use of analogies drawn from the Stoic philosophy of his day occurs in Chapter 12 of his *First Letter to the Corinthians*. In that letter he compares the organism of the body of Christ to that of the human body. 'For just as the body is one and has many members, and all the members of the body, though many, are one body, so it is with Christ. For the body does not consist of one member but of many'.[24] A not dissimilar idea occurs in one of Seneca's moral epistles. There he writes in his discussion of human relationships: 'All that you behold, that which comprises both god and man is one – we are the parts of one great body'.[25]

It is important to note that though Saint Paul employed the body analogy, he went well beyond Seneca in the use to which he put it. The idea of the church as the body of Christ is hardly Stoic. Rather, it

---

[19] *Wisdom of Solomon* 17.11.
[20] Seneca, *Epistles*, 16.
[21] Seneca, *Epistles*, 54.
[22] Epictetus, 1:4.
[23] Marcus Aurelius, *Meditations*, book I, section 9.
[24] 1 Cor. 12.12-14.
[25] Seneca, *Epistles*, 95, 52.

is being suggested that his teaching was less monolithic than certain passages quoted at the outset might suggest. Insistent though he was on the primacy of faith and of grace, it would be inaccurate to infer from this that his thinking was not influenced by the sort of general philosophical ideas by which he was surrounded, above all by the dominant thought model of his day – Later Stoicism – of which something has been said in Chapter 1.

The Apostolic Fathers

The earliest Christian writers outside the 27 books that make up the canon of the New Testament, Clement of Rome, Ignatius of Antioch, the Shepherd of Hermas and the *Didache* or *Teaching of the Twelve Apostles*, are conveniently grouped together and known as the Apostolic Fathers, a title given them since the later half of the seventeenth century. All of them wrote almost entirely for the benefit of fellow believers and seem to have concerned themselves very little with the pagan world around them. By and large, the writings of the Apostolic Fathers like those of the New Testament books were composed either for people who already believed, or for prospective converts, drawn above all from Judaism. This means that in so far as there was a coherent plan of evangelization, the earlier apologetic strategy evident above all from the sermons of Saint Peter at Acts 2, 3 and 4 and Stephen in Acts 7 was carried on by them. The Apostolic Fathers were interested in establishing the credibility and credentials of the gospel from the Old Testament from prophecy. In this they were doing little more than the 'stranger' who had met the two disciples on their way from Jerusalem.[26] Even so it needs to be stressed that the assumption underlying both Clement and Ignatius is that they were addressing people who were already of the household of the faith.

Clement of Rome

Clement of Rome wrote his *Letter to the Corinthians* towards the end of the first century AD or perhaps slightly earlier. The principle

---

[26]Lk. 24.27.

concern of the letter is the re-establishment of some measure of unity and order in the faction ridden Christian community of Corinth. The disunity so strongly censured by Clement was summed up under the general rubric of 'stasis' or dissension. The expression occurs nearly ten times in the *Letter*. In the opening section, he refers to the 'disgraceful and unholy sedition devised by a few headstrong persons'. Near the end of the *Letter*, he refers to the ungodly sedition that he hopes he has been an agent in suppressing.[27] It would appear that the basic source of the dissension was a rejection of the power and place of the leaders of the community, usually styled presbyters. The importance of the letter can be gauged by the fact that Eusebius tells us that in the middle of the second century, it was customary to read it in the church at Corinth.[28]

Clement's arguments in favour of harmony are drawn largely from the Old Testament, with occasional ones from the New Testament. Indeed it is not at all clear that he knew any New Testament writings aside from several letters of Saint Paul, and there, only the moral sections. The two Pauline letters which furnished him with arguments were above all those to the *Romans* and, not surprisingly, the *First Letter to the Corinthians*.

His appeal in Chapter 20 to the order of nature as a pattern for the order of the church has clear Stoic antecedents. Indeed the whole passage is not unlike Acts 17.24-31 in displaying the influence of Stoicizing Judaism on early Christian cosmology. Clement argues that the movement of the heavenly bodies and the rotation of the seasons take place under the general management of the divine order. 'The sun and the moon, the choirs of stars move harmoniously without any disturbance on their appointed course'.[29] The whole passage is heavily under the influence of the Hellenistic Jewish understanding of the world, of the type we find in the book of Sirach, where we read 'The Lord arranged his works in an eternal order and their dominion for all generations. They neither hunger nor grow weary'.[30] An even closer parallel can be found in Cicero's treatise *On the Nature of the Gods*, 'Who is there', he asks 'who can observe the fixed motions of the heavens and the established order

---

[27]Clement of Rome, *Letter to the Corinthians*, section 63.
[28]Eusebius, *Ecclesiastical History*, 4;23;11
[29]Clement, Chapter 20.
[30]Sirach, 16: 26 ff.

of the stars and not conclude that they are under the influence of the stars?'[31]

In Section 24 of the *Letter*, Clement reduces the resurrection to an example of the way in which day follows night. 'We behold a daily resurrection, Day and night show us resurrection. Night sleeps; day arises'.[32] This was a singularly popular illustration. We find Tertullian also making use of it: 'Day by day light is slain and shines once more; darkness in due turn departs and follows on again, and the dead stars come to life'.[33] Rather surprisingly, if we consider the peculiarly Christian character of the doctrine of the resurrection, we find Seneca using very similar language for the same purpose, he writes 'Death which we fear and shrink from merely interrupts life; the time will return, when we shall be restored to the light of day . . . Mark how the round of the universe repeats its course'[34] and more in the same vein. Useful though the illustrations are, they serve rather to erode the special significance of the event they illustrate.

A further area in which it is possible to see Clement taking over habits of thought whose home was initially outside the biblical tradition is that of the emotions of God. The problem emerges above all in the application of anger to God. We meet with the wrath of God often enough in the Old Testament. The creation of the golden calf by the Israelites provokes the divine wrath. 'And the Lord said to Moses, "Now, therefore, let me alone that my wrath may burn hot against them"'.[35] Later: 'Behold the name of the Lord comes from afar, burning with his anger and in thick rising smoke'.[36] Finally: 'In my anger a fire is enkindled which shall burn for ever'.[37] Although the New Testament has far less on this theme, it is by no means absent. Saint Paul had ascribed anger to God when he writes: 'For the wrath of God is revealed from heaven against all ungodliness'.[38] In the next chapter, he speaks of an Eschatological 'day of wrath'. But how, the philosopher asks, can we ascribe to God passions we are loath to ascribe to good people?

---

[31] Cicero, *On the Nature of the Gods*, 2: 38–97.
[32] Clement, *Letter*, 24.
[33] Tertullian, *Apology*, Chapter 48.
[34] Seneca, *Epistles*, 36.
[35] Exodus 32.
[36] Isa. 30.27.
[37] Jer. 17.4.
[38] Rom. 1.18.

There is no simple answer to this age old problem, which had vexed Plato.[39] The moral perfection of God seems to protect him from all irrational or immoral behaviour. But it is above all to Clement that we owe the first Christian affirmation of the superiority of God to anger and all passion. He writes: 'Let us see him with our intelligence and gaze upon him with the eyes of the soul and behold his patient plan. Let us reflect how free from anger he is in his dealing with the whole of his creation'.[40] This theme of the divine superiority to anger was taken up by Ignatius of Antioch[41] and, at a later date, by Athenagoras when he writes that 'the divine needs nothing and is above all desire'.[42]

At the same time, or even earlier, we find the same theme in non-Christian authors of roughly the same period. Horace, for example, tells us that anger is a brief form of madness.[43] We find the notion that absence of anger is a virtue in Stoics and Platonists alike. Seneca's identification of the human spirit with God means in effect that human and divine virtue will be identical: 'The wise man surveys and scorns all the possessions of others as calmly as does Jupiter'.[44] Both Epictetus and Marcus Aurelius censure anger. The former writes that: 'my enemy exercises my patience, my dispassionateness, my gentleness'[45] and at the opening of his *Meditations*, Marcus says: 'I learnt from my grandfather Verus a kindly disposition and sweetness of temper'.[46]

But while the Stoics recommended the effectual extirpation of passion, Aristotle and his second century AD followers advocated moderate use of the passions as of all things. Excess, writes the second century Middle Platonist, Alcinous, is to be avoided.[47] This divine freedom from anger is echoed in a Platonist writer of the middle second century, Apuleius of Madaura in his treatise *On Plato and his Teaching*.[48] Plotinus takes a more austere position

---

[39]Plato, *Republic*, book iv.
[40]Clement, *Letter to the Corinthians*, 19: 3.
[41]Ignatius of Antioch, *Letter to the Philadelphians* 1: 2.
[42]Athenagoras, *Embassy* 29: 3.
[43]Horace, *letter* I 2: 62.
[44]Seneca, *Epistles* 73: 14.
[45]Epictetus, *Discourses*, book 3, xx: 9.
[46]Marcus, *Meditations*.
[47]Alcinous, *Handbook*, Chapter 30.
[48]Apuleius of Madaura, *On Plato and his Teaching*, 2: 4.

when he assumes that the immortal and the imperishable must be impassive.[49] *Apatheia* is preferable to *metriopatheia*. The whole subject has been extensively treated by Max Pohlenz in his Gottingen dissertation for 1909 entitled *Vom Zorne Gottes* or *On the Divine Anger*. His invaluable monograph is designed to establish the thesis that the Stoic influence on the biblical idea of God resulted in the evisceration of the latter. The problem became particularly acute in the Christological controversies of the fifth century, where the question arose how could anger, or any form of weakness, be attributed to the divine as distinct from the human nature of Christ. To the apparently simple question: 'Could God die or could he suffer or could he be angry or sad?', it was hard to provide a satisfactory or convincing answer without dividing Christ or attributing to the divine features he did not or could not possess. The above account of Clement's *Letter* shows us that even though he was addressing a Christian audience on internal business, he used patterns of thought which had a home outside the church.

Ignatius of Antioch

In Ignatius the Martyr, Bishop of Antioch, who died in Rome in about 107 AD, there is far less evidence of Stoic or indeed of any other philosophic influence. On his way to Rome to suffer martyrdom during the reign of the emperor Trajan, he wrote seven letters in which the most important areas treated are the unity of the church under the threefold ministry of bishop, priest and deacon, and in contrast with the Docetists, the reality of Christ's humanity. In the *Letter to the Ephesians*, he writes of the three mysteries: 'the virginity of Mary, the reality of her giving birth, and of the death of the Lord'.[50]

The final mystery made a deep impression upon him as is clear from the *Letter to the Romans*. So emphatic on one occasion was his insistence on the reality of the sufferings of Christ that he wrote: 'Allow me to become an imitator of the suffering of my God'.[51] Such a sentiment would be improbable in Clement. Ignatius' exaggerated

---

[49] Plotinus, *Enneads* book I, 1: 2.
[50] Ignatius of Antioch, *Letter to the Ephesians*, section 19.
[51] Ignatius of Antioch, *Letter to the Romans*, 6: 3.

passion for martyrdom is well known and figures largely in his letter to the church in Rome, where he writes: 'My love is crucified and I have no longer in me a fire that is in love with matter'.[52] None of these topics can look to Hellenism as a possible source except, perhaps the highly rhetorical way in which the subjects are treated.

There are some possible references to the mystery religions. Above all, he urges the Ephesians to assemble in complete harmony with the bishop and presbyters for the Eucharist, 'breaking one bread which is the medicine of immortality, the antidote against dying'.[53] Apart from the idea of breaking one bread which we find in Chapter 2 of the Acts of the Apostles, the rest of the language is very unusual. The word translated 'antidote' occurs nowhere in the New Testament, while the expression *pharmakos* means poisoner in the Apocalypse 21: 8. The more positive meaning, that the sacrament communicates immortality, though reflecting the thought of the Eucharistic discourse of John 6, owes much to the language of the mystery religions which often climaxed in a sacred meal. Ritual meals formed an important part of the cult of Mithra. The similarities between Mithra and the gospel had been remarked as early as about 140 by Justin[54] and later in about 173 AD by Celsus.[55] Even though the dependence of the Christian mysteries on the Greek is doubted, it still remains true that both sides believed in the importance and possibility of communion with God through a common meal.

The Apologists

From the middle of the second century AD, the situation with respect to the possibility of a marriage between faith and philosophy had begun to alter. Although Paul occasionally uses 'foreign' ideas to reinforce his point, this is done rhetorically rather than philosophically: he does at least use Stoic expressions. The Apostolic Fathers, Clement above all, in the same way, as we have

---

[52]Ignatius of Antioch, *Letter to the church in Rome*.
[53]Ignatius of Antioch, *Letter to the Ephesians*, 20.
[54]Justin, *Apology* 1: 66.
[55]As recorded by Origen in *Against Celsus* 1: 9 and 6: 22.

seen, on occasion borrow expressions from their non-Christian contemporaries. The Apologists, above all Justin and Tertullian go considerably further. Yet though they may use philosophical ideas with which to reinforce or illustrate their position, they make no attempt to bring them into a coherent system. Origen in the third century was the first to attempt such a move. Over and above this, it also needs to be remembered that the actual attitude to 'foreign' culture was by no means monochrome. Some like Justin were amazingly positive towards it. A little later in the same century we find a markedly different approach from writers like Tatian and Tertullian, both of them his pupils.

Before any more precise account of the ideas of the Apologists is given, a brief definition will help. An apologist, standing in the tradition first expressed by Plato in his *Apology of Socrates* offers a defence of his deeds and words in the manner of a barrister in a law court. Cardinal Newman did much the same in 1864 with the publication of his *Apologia pro vita sua*. But at the same time as offering a defence, he also endeavours to establish the basic truthfulness of his own position. Christianity can meet all the highest demands of the critic. The particular critics envisaged by Justin and Tertullian were the Roman government and the pagan intelligentsia of their day.

Justin Martyr

Justin Martyr was born at Nablus, modern Sychar in Samaria, at the beginning of the second century AD, and was martyred in Rome in 165. He himself tells us in his *Dialogue with Trypho* that he began life as a philosopher ending up as a Platonist, passing by Aristotle on the way. Even after his conversion to Christianity, he regarded Christianity as 'the true philosophy' and continued to make use of the philosopher's cloak[56] and is described as 'a genuine lover of the true philosophy'.[57] He had come to the gospel through various schools of philosophy and was never ungrateful enough to despise the ladder that had enabled him to ascend even higher than Plato. He is both positive and eclectic in his attitude. He tries to

---

[56] Eusebius, *Ecclesiastical History* iv, 11: 8.
[57] *Historia Ecclesiastica* HE iv, 8: 3.

divorce ancient religion and philosophy and then affect a 'marriage' between the gospel and Platonism – an approach which the pagan Celsus and many non-Christian later writers deeply resented, as they did all attempts to use Plato for evangelical purposes. It is indeed arguable that the closer connection we find between Greek religion and philosophy was a reaction in part against the type of division proposed by Justin.

The optimism of Justin is everywhere evident. All serious seekers after truth, men of the stature of Heraclitus and of Socrates, he tells us were Christians even before Christ[58] – a view that none of his contemporaries and few of his followers seem to have shared. The true philosopher owed what truth he possessed to the presence within of the seminal reason or seed word[59] – an expression which owes something to Stoicism. Christ is, for Justin, the whole word, of which we share a part.[60]

Marcus Aurelius, the Stoic emperor and a rough contemporary of Justin uses the same expression: 'Thou hast subsisted as part of the whole. Thou shalt vanish into that which begat thee, or rather thou shalt be taken again into its seminal reason, by a process of change'.[61] It was clearly intended to account for the possession by quite different races of the same basic ideas. Plato had used the theory of pre-existence and of forms to account for the same phenomenon. Saint Augustine appealed to memory. And yet despite this generous attitude, Justin also insists that the ultimate criterion of truth is Christ and his teaching. He writes rather ambiguously that despite the similarity between Plato and Christ the two are not identical. 'Whatever has been well said by them belongs to us as Christians'.[62]

Justin, however, does not always treat his subject in the same way. Although at times he will appeal to some general notions to explain similarities, on other occasions he appeals to a counter theory that used the theory of borrowing. So, for example, the account of creation in Plato's *Timaeus*[63] is, according to Justin,[64]

---

[58] Justin, *First Apology*, 46.
[59] Justin, *Second Apology*, 8: 13.
[60] Justin, *Second Apology*, 10.
[61] Marcus Aurelius, *Meditations*, book iv, 14.
[62] Justin, *Second Apology*, 13.
[63] Plato, *Timaeus*, 30.
[64] Justin, *First Apology*, 59.

derived from the first chapter of Genesis. In Chapter 60 of the same treatise he argues that the Platonic idea in *Timaeus* 36 of a great X stretched over the world is derived (rather improbably) via Moses from the cross and the Trinity. At a later date Augustine corrected his belief that Plato depended on Jeremiah, whom he was said to have met in Egypt.[65]

But it is for his *logos* theology that Justin is best known. Starting as he did from a very exalted view of the divine nature, which was ingenerate and beyond the reach of human speech and comprehension, he has to bring this remote and somewhat abstract figure into relationship with the world. He needed a sort of bridge or go-between God to link our spatial and temporal existence with the unseen God. This role Justin assigned to the *logos* or the Word. This *logos* was the agent of God in the creation and redemption of the world. He is a sort of intermediary God, not quite as exalted as the mysterious Father but much greater than the created order. Much of later theology wrestled with this idea and was forced to face the question as to where the Word belonged: was it a creature or was it a creator?

The provenance of this idea in Justin has not yet been satisfactorily settled. One of the most obvious sources of the idea is the prologue of the fourth gospel. Unfortunately it is never cited despite the fact that Justin does seem to have known the fourth gospel, as in Chapter 61 we find a clear quotation from Jn 3.3-5: 'Unless you be born from above you shall not enter the kingdom of heaven'. Philo has also been proposed as a source. The structure of their respective systems is very similar above all in his treatise *On the making of the world*. Philo identifies the incorporeal world with the divine Reason,[66] which thus becomes the agent and pattern for the creation of the visible world. But Philo is never mentioned by Justin.

Some brand of second century Platonism has also been proposed, but examples of the use of the *logos* ideas by them are not easily found, except perhaps in Plutarch's treatise *On Isis and Osiris*. It is clear, therefore that the idea of some form of mediator between the divine realm and the material order was held by many different writers of the first and second centuries AD. But whatever its precise provenance, the *logos* theology contained certain obvious

[65]Augustine, *City of God*, 8: 11.
[66]Philo, *On the making of the world*, 10: 36.

disadvantages. As Henry Chadwick observes, by subordinating the Word/Son to the very remote Father God this argument, 'led with a virtually irresistible force straight to Arianism'.[67] Justin's sympathetic attitude to Hellenism was shared by other Apologists like Aristides and Quadratus who endeavoured to establish the antiquity and thereby the truth of the gospel. But it was by no means the only response. The influence of the anti-intellectualism of 1 Corinthians i and ii can be seen in two other second century writers, Tatian and Tertullian.

Tatian

Tatian was a native of Assyria and flourished in the second third of the second century and appears to have acquired, according to Eusebius, a considerable reputation for learning. According to Irenaeus,[68] Tatian arrived in Rome where he became a pupil of Justin Martyr, for whom he clearly cherished a great reverence, calling him 'the most admirable Justin'.[69] However, he seems not to have shared his master's optimism and positive attitude to Greek thought. In about 150 or 172 AD, Tatian returned to the east and broke away from the church in order to join the sect of the Encratites who insisted on the importance of extreme asceticism and took a very hostile view to all sorts of sexual activity even inside marriage.

The main thrust of his work, *Oration against the Greeks*, was to establish the greater antiquity of the Hebrew scriptures over the Greeks – an interesting line of defence, which died only slowly and was used to account for the undeniable similarities between the bible and Greek philosophy. Tatian hoped to prove that since the bible was more ancient than the philosophy of the Greeks, Christianity is more profound and more venerable than any Greek system and consequently also truer. We have seen Justin employing this line of argument in dealing with creation, the cross and the Trinity. Even Saint Augustine employed this approach[70] when he argued that Plato depended on Jeremiah, whom he was said to have met on a

---

[67]H. Chadwick, *Early Christian Thought and the Classical Tradition*, p. 16.
[68]Cited by Eusebius in *Ecclesiastical History* iv, 39.
[69]Tatian, *Oratio ad Graecos*, Chapter 18.
[70]Augustine, in a celebrated passage in his *On Christian Teaching* 2, xxvii: 43.

visit to Egypt. Augustine subsequently withdrew this position, even so, the desire to establish the greater antiquity of the gospel and, within that, of orthodoxy was a mainstay of many an argument. 'Nothing could be both new and true at the same time'.

Chapter 2 of *Oration against the Greeks* contains, among other things, a violent attack on Greek civilization: on Plato for his gluttony and even more so on Aristotle – never a favourite among the Fathers – both for his restriction of providence to the superlunary sphere and for his fawning attitude to his pupil, Alexander the Great. Tatian writes as follows:

> Aristotle, after ignorantly setting a limit to providence and defining happiness in terms of his own pleasures, used to fawn in a very uncultured way on that wild young man, Alexander, who in true Aristotelian fashion shut his own friend up in a cage, because he refused to prostrate himself . . . His modern disciples [that is those of Aristotle] are good for a laugh; they exclude providence from any part in sublunary affairs . . . that provide the care that providence fails to give! And those who have neither beauty nor wealth nor physical strength, nor good birth, these according to Aristotle, have no happiness. Let men like this go on with their philosophising.[71]

It is not at all clear what sources Tatian had for some of his more outrageous statements. Some can be paralleled in the *Lives of the Philosophers* by Diogenes Laertius, but not the cage story.

The frequency with which denial of divine providence is attributed to Aristotle by the Fathers is quite striking. It is a natural inference from his definition of God as the object of desire and as self thinking thought, which cannot have interest in or concern for anything or anyone below himself. Tatian's vitriolic hostility to Hellenism may make his attack on Aristotle intelligible, but Origen's bald statement of the same truth[72] reinforces the view that the effective denial of divine providence was felt as a feature of Aristotle's thought by many articulate Christians. Gregory of Nazianzus in his first *Theological Oration*[73] maintains something similar.

---

[71]Tatian, *Oration against the Greeks*.
[72]Origen, *Contra Celsum* 1: 21.
[73]Gregory of Nazianzus, *First Theological Oration*, section 10.

Even so, despite his at times vitriolic attitude to Greek philosophy, it would be quite unfair to assume either that Tatian was wholly ignorant of it or that he was untouched by it. His account of the divine nature[74] contains expressions which would be quite at home in a moderate Platonist of the latter half of the second century. His insistence on the eternity and spirituality of God commits him to a view of the divine nature not far distant from that of Alcinous. He writes: 'Our God has no origin in time, since he alone is without beginning and himself is the beginning of all things . . . He is invisible and impalpable and we know him through his creation'.[75] Then follows a quotation from Rom. 1.20: 'What is invisible in his power, we comprehend through what he has made'. There is nothing very striking here. Tatian distinguishes his position from that of the Stoics by his insistence that the statement 'God is spirit'[76] does not mean that God pervades matter. Clearly Tatian knew something of the current philosophical scene and was selective in his treatment of it.

Tertullian

Tertullian from Carthage is undoubtedly the most exciting figure to emerge from the Western church of the second and third centuries. His influence upon Western theology has been considerable. Jerome tells us that Cyprian, the martyr bishop of Carthage in the mid third century – he died in 258 in the persecution of Valerian – referred to him as 'The Master',[77] and that never a day passed without reading him. The theological vocabulary of Tertullian was subsequently adopted by Hilary, Augustine and Leo, that of the last named was canonized at the Council of Chalcedon in 451. Yet he has never been very popular with the chattering classes. Gibbon refers to him as 'the zealous African'[78] – Matthew Arnold as 'the fierce Tertullian',[79] while more recently, E. R. Dodds speaks of his 'venomous fanaticism'.[80]

---

[74]Tatian, *Oration against the Greeks*, Chapter 4.
[75]Tatian, *Oration against the Greeks*.
[76]Jn 4.24.
[77]Jerome, *On Illustrious Men*, Chapter 53 [=PL 23;663].
[78]E. Gibbon, *The History of the Decline and fall of the Roman Empire*, Chapter 13.
[79]M. Arnold, *Literature and Dogma* (1873).
[80]E. R. Dodds, *Pagans and Christians in an age of Anxiety* (Cambridge University Press, 1965).

Tertullian was converted to Christianity towards the end of the second century, before 197 AD. The character of North African Christianity prior to this date is hard to ascertain due to lack of evidence, though in all probability some of the New Testament already existed in its Old Latin dress two centuries before Jerome began producing his *Vulgate* at the request of Pope Damasus in 384. Tertullian probably trained as an orator and perhaps also as a lawyer though, despite the witness of Jerome, he was never ordained a priest.

Then, in the beginning of the next century, in about 207 AD, he distanced himself from the Catholic Church in North Africa and joined the sect of the Montanists, a spirit inspired group that began life in about 173 in central Asia Minor In this movement, Montanus, its founder, had the support of two women prophets, Maximilla and Priscilla. They and their followers endeavoured to inject a degree of charismatic enthusiasm into a church that, they believed, had lost its initial spiritual character in its increasing attention to the importance of doctrines and church structures. The movement, with its appeal to the charismatic spirit of the early church, raised acutely the whole question of the place of both the Holy Spirit and of the mind in religion. As we shall see when the attitude of Origen to the action of the Holy Spirit is discussed, it was precisely this attribution to the Holy Spirit of irrationalism that Origen so strongly rejected.

It must be stressed, however, that there seems to have been nothing unorthodox in the movement. Their most distinctive feature was their apocalyptic and Millenarian approach. They looked forward to the descent of the heavenly Jerusalem near Pepuza in Phrygia. All this may account for Eusebius of Caesarea's rather hostile account of the movement in his *Ecclesiastical History*.[81]

This Asia Minor movement spread to North Africa later in the same century, and to it in its African incarnation Tertullian added his peculiar gifts in about 207 AD. It is not surprising that Tertullian committed himself to this sect, it being an expression of the zeal and austerity that marked his personality and whole approach and led him to condemn among other abuses the current penitential system as too lax. Even so it would be a mistake to suppose that his commitment to the new movement meant for Tertullian a death of interest in theological issues. His treatises *On the Incarnation* also

---

[81]Eusebius, *Ecclesiastsical History*, 5: 16.

called *On the Flesh of Christ* and *Against Praxeas* certainly date from his Montanist period.

Tertullian is often depicted as the prophet of irrationalism. In a famous outburst consciously reminiscent of the opening of Saint Paul's *First Letter to the Corinthians*, he writes: 'What indeed has Athens to do with Jerusalem? What has the Academy to do with the Church? . . . We want no curious disputation after possessing Christ Jesus.'[82] The whole argument is designed to prove that philosophy is the parent of heresy, a view with which many of the Fathers verbally expressed sympathy, while at the same time introducing philosophy by the back door. Similarly, he uses language very like that of Tatian to belabour Aristotle and Plato, writing:

> The same Aristotle's shameful tutorship of Alexander is equivalent to flattery. Plato, no better, fawns upon Dionysius to gratify his belly. But what have the philosopher and Christian in common, the disciple of Greece and the disciple of heaven – the business of the one with the reputation of the other with salvation . . . the thief of truth and its guardian?'.[83]

On one occasion he goes so far as to claim that all heresies – he has in mind principally Gnosticism – arise from philosophy, writing: 'Valentinus was a Platonist'.[84] Yet it is worth noting that this anti-Platonist stance does not include Stoicism within its scope. As we have seen, Seneca was something of a favourite with Tertullian and is cited by him in the last chapter of the same work, the *Apologeticus*, which contains the slurs on the private characters of Plato and Aristotle.

Again his supposed fondness for a paradox is often inferred from an inaccurate quotation from section 5 his work *On the Flesh of Christ* or *On the Incarnation* , where he is said to have written: 'I believe because it is absurd'. What he actually wrote was less strident: 'The Son of God was crucified: I am not ashamed – because it is shameful. The Son of God died: it is at once credible because it is silly. He was buried and rose again: it is certain – because it is impossible'.[85] This is not quite the gospel of unreason, but comes

---

[82]Tertullian, *On the Prescription of Heretics*, 7.
[83]Tertullian, *Apologeticus* 46, 15.
[84]Tertullian, *On the Prescription of Heretics*.
[85]Tertullian, *On the Flesh of Christ*.

close to it. The difficulty with it is that we need a further criterion in our search for religious faith than simply paradox. We know there are both good and false or bad paradoxes, how are we to decide between the two without invoking an external criterion? Henry Chadwick writes 'Tertullian's interest here is to preserve the distinctiveness of faith, to prevent it from being absorbed within a suffocating system of metaphysical speculation where it has no room to breathe'.[86] This may account for his subsequent sympathy with Montanism.

However, to suggest that Tertullian is to be treated simply as a prophet of irrationalism, a sort of antecedent of *The Imitation of Christ* of Søren Kierkegaard is a gross oversimplification. Not infrequently, he is content to employ language drawn from Stoicism with which to explore and give some sort of system to the gospel. His attachment to the Stoa finds unexpected expression in his open admiration for Seneca, whom he cites with approval several times and on at least one occasion as 'Our Seneca'.[87] On such occasions as this, he clearly thinks of philosophy as an ally rather than as an enemy. In *Apology*, while applauding the correct thinking of Seneca and others on the need for endurance, he adds the comment that: 'their words never find so many disciples as the Christians win, who teach by their deeds'.[88]

Even in more specifically doctrinal areas he makes use of language and images drawn from philosophy, above all from Stoicism, still the dominant philosophy of the day. This is very clear in his treatise *Against Praxeas*, written in his Montanist period some time after 206. In this work, he exploits words like *substantia*, *persona* and mixture with which to give expression to the mystery of the Trinity and of the Incarnation and, in so doing, lays the foundation for standard Western theological vocabulary. The expressions have a Stoic background. His central concern in this treatise was to oppose the Modalism of the mysterious and otherwise unknown Praxeas. According to Tertullian in Chapter 1 of his treatise, Praxeas 'put to flight the Spirit and crucified the Father'[89] so denying any real distinction of persons in the godhead. This encounter afforded

---

[86]H. Chadwick, *Early Christian Thought and the Classical Tradition*, p. 2.
[87]Tertullian, *On the Soul*, Chapter 20.
[88]Tertullian, *Apology*, Chapter 50.
[89]Tertullian, *Against Praxeas*, 1.

Tertullian an opportunity that helped him forge the Latin theological vocabulary with its emphasis upon the unity of the substance of God in language found later in Augustine.

It has even been argued, though not entirely persuasively, that it is to Tertullian through Ossius, Bishop of Cordoba, that we owe the presence in the Nicene Creed of the word 'substance'. Tertullian's language of 'substance' may indeed be echoed by the consubstantial of the creed, but his understanding of the word is materialistic, in which he differs from the creedal meaning.

Again Tertullian's language of mixture and of the united but distinct character of the status of divine and human in Christ, occurs in several places. In his *Apologeticus* 21, he writes: 'Christ is man mingled with God'. Tertullian's adoption of Stoic language was not uncritical. In *Against Praxeas* Tertullian questions such talk and rejects the notion that the divine and human in Christ unite to form a sort of mixture, like electrum, where neither element remains unchanged. He writes: 'We observe [sc. in Christ] a double quality [duplex status], not confused but combined, Jesus in one person, God and man'.[90] This idea can be discovered in the writings of Leo the Great,[91] above all in the tome endorsed at Chalcedon in 451. 'To such a degree there remained unimpaired the proper being of each substance'.[92]

We find in Tertullian, therefore, a healthy tension between the rejection and use of reason in Christianity. As von Campenhausen points out in *The Fathers of the Latin Church*, Tertullian demands less a sacrifice of the intellect than an appropriate restriction of intellectual hubris or pride.[93] For him, also, what is important in religion is truth rather than tradition. He readily concedes to his pagan and Jewish critics that at least in 200 AD, antiquity was not a mark of the gospel. 'We are but of yesterday' he writes 'and yet we have filled everything'.[94] His appeal therefore is not, as it was later to become in writers like Eusebius, to antiquity but to success.

A further and even more telling element in his general apologetic is his appeal to truth. This latter point is made clear in the first

---

[90]Tertullian, *Against Praxeas*, Chapter 27.

[91]Pope from 440–461.

[92]Leo's Tome of Leo section 3. p. 338 Creeds, Councils and Controversies Edited by J. Stevenson 1966.

[93]von Campenhausen, *The Fathers of the Latin Church*.

[94]Tertullian, *Apology* 37: 4.

chapter of his treatise *On the Veiling of Virgins*, where he writes with reference to Jn 14.6: 'I am the truth' that 'Our Lord Christ described himself not as custom but as the truth . . . Whatever opposes the truth is heresy, even though it be ancient custom'.[95] We find similar assertions of the truth element in Christianity in his *Apology*, written in about 200 AD. There we find him writing: 'Christians are worshippers of the Truth'.[96] Later, he writes: 'You by your worship of a lie, by your neglect of the true religion of the true God – and more than that – by your assault upon it, commit against the true God, the crime of real irreligion'.[97] Finally Tertullian writes: 'That is the rule of truth which comes from Christ'.[98]

Tertullian's willingness to defend his position as if in a law court reinforces the point that he is treating the religion he has embraced as more than either a system of ritual or as a system of morals, or indeed as something so paradoxical that accepting the gospel means saying farewell to reason. On the contrary the gospel offers truth about God because it is essentially a *religio veritatis*, a religion of truth. In *On the Incarnation* he writes: 'Why make out that Christ was half a lie? He was wholly the truth'.[99] His followers, therefore, need to expound and defend its views at the bar of intelligent spectators. Philosophers, above all men like 'Our Seneca', can be very valuable in this programme, but revelation has the first and the last word. Belief in the doctrines of the Trinity and Incarnation are capable of rational defence and interpretation.

[95]Tertullian, *On the veiling of virgins*.
[96]Tertullian, *Apology* 15: 8.
[97]Tertullian, *Apology* 24.
[98]Tertullian, *Apology* 47: 10.
[99]Tertullian, *On the Incarnation*, Chapter 5.

3

The Alexandrian school[1]

Judaism and philosophy in Alexandria

The diffidence sometimes expressed by Saint Paul on the place of philosophy in his newly found faith in Christ was not restricted to him as we have seen. Even so it is dangerous to argue from him (and from those who seem to share his point of view) that strident opposition to the claims of rational thought within the early church existed. In this connection it is important to remember that the 'contamination' of religion by philosophy existed in Alexandrian Judaism in the first century BC if not earlier. It goes back to the beginning of the third century if not earlier with the Septuagint, the Greek translation of the Old Testament. This owed its production to the initiative of Ptolemy Philadelphus (285–246 BC). It was probably completed by the middle of the second century BC and it is from this translation, often abbreviated to LXX, that the New Testament writers commonly quoted the bible.

It included several texts not to be found in the Hebrew of the Old Testament, above all the so called Sapiential books or Books of Wisdom, notably Ecclesiaticus or *Sirach* and the *Book of Wisdom*. The influence of philosophy, especially of Stoicism, upon these is patent. So we find at *Sir.* 43.27 the arresting statement 'He is the All'. The absolute of philosophy has been identified with the personal God. In *Wisdom* we are told that the whole of the created order is held together by a controlling spirit,[2] and in language which is echoed by Rom. 1.20 ff., we read: 'From the size and

---

[1] Bigg, 1913; Chadwick, 1966.
[2] *Wis.* 1.7.

beauty of the created order, the author of it all is perceived'.[3] A little earlier, a Platonic note is struck when we read that 'that almighty hand of God shaped the world out of shapeless matter'.[4] These passages simply serve to illustrate the fact that, as we have seen in the preceding chapter, large parts of the *Book of Wisdom* show philosophic influence.

At the turn of the millennium, Alexandrian Judaism produced a figure of great importance in Philo (25 BC–50 AD). His absorption of current philosophical ideas, above all from renascent Platonism, may well have influenced both the Prologue to the fourth gospel with its use of the central notion of *logos*, the Letter to the Hebrews, and the writings of Justin Martyr. Philo's influence upon Clement of Alexandria is much more certain. For Philo, the Old Testament scripture, above all in matters of physics and ethics, was a vast cryptogram, in which under the form of the historical narrative there lurked deeper meanings waiting to be discovered by the intelligent inquirer. What the *Homeric Allegories* of Heraclitus did for Homer at roughly the same period, Philo did for the bible. The work of conflating biblical imagery with Hellenistic philosophy, already begun in the Sapiential books, was greatly enriched by Philo. The basic motive of both writers was similar, namely to show that the sacred books of both Greece and Israel had contemporary relevance and were able to shed valuable light on problems of both morality and metaphysics. One of the principal motives for the efforts both of the translators of the LXX and of Philo was to demonstrate to their fellow citizens in the university city of Alexandria that belief in the revelation of God to the Jews did not mean cultural isolation.

Further to that, Philo harnessed a form of Platonized Stoicism to the interpretation of the biblical narrative. His account of the divine nature was greatly enhanced by the idea of the divine incomprehensibility, which he either invented himself or, more probably, took over from contemporary exegesis of Plato's *Timaeus*. There Plato writes: 'It is hard to know and impossible to tell the truth about God'.[5] In this he is echoed by Cicero.[6]

---

[3] *Wis.* 13.5.
[4] *Wis.* 11.17.
[5] Plato, *Timaeus*, 28c.
[6] Cicero, *On the Nature of the Gods*, book I, Chapter 30.

Philo, who is arguably more emphatic than Cicero in his assertion of the non-availability of the divine to mortal eyes and minds, fuses with this a mediating Word and so was able to construct a cosmology which possibly underlies the prologue of the fourth gospel and Col. 1.15. In his treatise *On the Creation of the World*, Philo situates the incorporeal world of forms within the divine reason or Word.[7] Perhaps intentionally, Philo has identified the active Word of God of Stoic provenance with the Platonic world of ideas. The Word of God now becomes the place of forms and bears a family likeness to Plotinus' location of the world of forms in the second hypostasis of the Mind or Spirit at *Ennead* 5, 1: 5.

Philo stands out not only because of the extent of his knowledge of and willingness to adopt and adapt later Hellenistic philosophy, but also because of the influence he exercised upon later Christian authors. Indeed his familiarity with and use of ideas drawn from contemporary philosophy is far more extensive than is that of later writers, Christian or otherwise. For, although it is indeed true that the majority of them show some acquaintance with Greek thought and ideas, they cannot be said to have fully ingested it into their systems as he did.

The subsequent influence of Philo in the church rather than in Judaism was immense. He was known and cited sometimes without acknowledgement.[8] His work *On Dreams* is praised by Origen, who writes: 'Philo also composed a book about this ladder (that is Jacob's ladder at Gen. 28.12-13), which is worthy of intelligent and wise study by those who wish to find the truth'.[9]

Eusebius of Caesarea writing in the first quarter of the fourth century was also well acquainted with Philo's writings as can be seen from his lengthy quotations both in his *Ecclesiastical History*[10] – an extract from Philo's account of the *Therapeutae* or Jewish contemplatives – and even more so in his *Preparation for the Gospel*. In this work Philo is quoted for his teaching on the second god or Word,[11] while xi:24 contains a large extract from the earlier sections of Philo's treatise *On the Making of the World*,

---

[7]Philo, *On the creation of the World*, 10: 36.
[8]Clement of Alexandria, *Stromata* 1: 23.
[9]Origen, *Against Celsus* 6: 21.
[10]Eusebius, *Ecclesiastical History*, ii, 17.
[11]Eusebius, *Preparation for the Gospel*, vii, 13.

a work which almost certainly exercised a profound, though again unacknowledged influence on Justin's cosmology. Eusebius cites vi:24–x:36 with occasional omissions. The passage deals with Philo's treatment of the opening words of the bible: 'In the beginning God made the heaven and the earth'. 'The entire world', Philo writes, 'is a copy of the divine image and it is manifest that the archetypal seal would be . . . the very Word of God'.[12] In other words the Word of God mediates between the remote God and the image of the image which we perceive in the visible universe.

All this means that nascent Christianity did not grow up in a world totally isolated from the influences of contemporary culture. Indeed the existence of a Greek-speaking community in the Decapolis region at the period of Christ's public ministry and mentioned twice by Mark[13] would have made such lack of communication hard to maintain even if it were desirable.

But was there in any event, as some have argued, a great difference between Alexandrian and Palestinian Judaism? This is a recurrent difficulty. It arises from a natural enough perception that Judaism in Alexandria was almost compelled to embark on a course of Hellenization, whereas no such demand existed in Palestine. Martin Hengel has questioned this somewhat facile distinction in his *The Hellenization of Judaea in the First Century AD*.[14] This book helps to dispel the view, once current, that there existed a great gulf between the Hellenized Judaism of Alexandria and the sort which flourished in Judaea itself.

Further both by name and by his being a sort of link figure between the Greeks and the rest of the apostles, one of the twelve was probably a Greek, Philip. It was to him we are told, that some Greeks came with the request: 'Sir, we should like to see Jesus'.[15] Once it is accepted that there was less of a gap between Jesus and Greece than some writers have supposed, it is much harder to sustain the assumption of great scholars like Harnack that the growth of Christianity, above all as it expressed itself in creed and worship, represented a sort of betrayal of the simple gospel of the Jewish Jesus in favour of the Greek spirit, perceived as an alien growth.

---

[12]Eusebius, vi 24–x: 36.
[13]Mk 5.20 and Mk 7.31.
[14]M. Hengel, *The Hellenization of Judaea in the First Century AD*.
[15]Jn 12.20.

Clement of Alexandria

Little can be said for certain about the life of Clement of Alexandria. Together with Philo and Origen, he is classed as one of the Platonists of Alexandria. He was in all probability a native of Athens and came to Alexandria from which he fled during the persecution of Septimius Severus in 202. In order to justify this behaviour, he is said to have employed a text from Saint Matthew's gospel: 'If they persecute in one city flee to another'.[16] His avoidance of martyrdom contrasts him with Origen who earnestly sought it. Clement's flight probably deprived him of being venerated as a saint.

He survives as the author of *Protrepticus* or *Exhortation to the Greeks*, an introduction to the study of the true philosophy that is Christianity. Like Justin before him, he tried to show the gospel as the supreme evidence of the activity of the light of the Word in the world in this charming work. It is a literary production, using ideas garnered primarily from classical literature but also from philosophy. In this he differs from Justin, who restricts his citations and references to philosophical writers. The opening sentence of Clement's work makes reference to two legendary minstrels, Amphion and Arion. 'Amphion of Thebes and Arion of Methymna were both minstrels'.[17] The language with which he addresses Christ as the light is very colourful and rich: 'O truly sacred mysteries, O pure light! In the blaze of the torches I have a vision of heaven and of God'.[18]

He also composed a three volume work entitled *The Pedagogue*, and another in eight volumes called the *Miscellanies* or *Carpet Bags* and a short treatise *On what rich man can be saved*, a liberal exegesis of Jesus' encounter with the rich young man in Mk 10.17-22. His central aim in that work is to show that wealth, like intelligence, is not of itself a diriment impediment to a serious following of the gospel. For Clement, what matters above all is not what you possess but the attitude you adopt toward possessions. Greed is not the prerogative of the rich. The central thrust of Chapter 12 is that the command of Jesus means 'strip the soul of passions'. The actual possession of wealth need not mean an attachment to money any more than an absence of possessions need mean an absence of

---

[16]Mt. 10.23.
[17]Clement, *Exhortation to the Greeks*.
[18]Clement, *Exhortation to the Greeks*, Chapter xii.

desire for wealth. The noblest command is given a distinctly Stoic interpretation. This little work has received a somewhat scornful critique from those who regard it as having deprived the gospel of its noblest appeal to contempt of consequence. But we need to remember that many thoughtful and wealthy Christians of his day were finding the elitism of the Gnostics more sympathetic to their intellectual tastes than the stress on poverty and simplicity that the New Testament often seems to invite.

As Chadwick points out, Clement insisted that philosophy was a divine gift, whose denial meant to deny both divine providence and the image of God in creation.[19] The same point is made by Pope John Paul II in *Fides et Ratio*,[20] where several passages from Clement's *Miscellanies* are cited in favour of the proposition that the Gospel is the true philosophy. The extremely close similarity existing, at least in Clement's mind, between the faith and alien wisdom is well illustrated by a passage quoted in the encyclical: 'Philosophy yearns for the wisdom that consists in rightness of soul and speech and uprightness of life . . . We call the philosophers among us those who love the wisdom which created all things and which teaches the knowledge of the Son of God.'[21] Faith does not demand an abandonment of intelligence.

The idea that Christianity is the true philosophy is already visible in Justin Martyr and persisted for a long time and we find it frequently in the writings of the Cappadocian Fathers, notably in Basil and Gregory of Nyssa, though with them the actual term philosophy is applied not so much to the academic pursuit of truth as to the serious pursuit of gospel values, above all as it finds expression in the monastic life.

Origen

'It has been well said of Origen', writes Archbishop Williams, 'that in him the "disciple of Jesus" coexists very uneasily with the Platonic speculative philosopher'.[22] The truth of this statement

---

[19] H. Chadwick, *Early Christian Thought and the Classical Tradition*, p. 43.
[20] Pope John Paul II, *Fides et Ratio*, p. 38.
[21] Clement, *Miscellanies*, 6: 7.
[22] Williams, *The Wound of Knowledge*, p. 39.

is well illustrated from a brief survey of his life, about which we are unusually well informed by Eusebius in the sixth book of his *Ecclesiastical History*.

Like Philo, and like Clement before him, the cradle of Origen's thought and life was Alexandria. But unlike them he was born of Christian parents in about 185 AD and narrowly escaped death (through his mother's efforts) in the persecution of Septimius Severus in 202. He became head of the Catechetical School of Alexandria and devoted himself to the study and explanation of scripture. He finally died at Caesarea in Palestine in 254, whither he had been exiled by his bishop Demetrius in about 231. Unfortunately for himself and for his posthumous reputation he was deprived of the crown of martyrdom on several occasions beside that of 202, notably during the persecution of Maximinus Thrax in 235 and that of Decius in 250 in the course of which he underwent violent tortures for his faith.

The gulf that separates Origen from Clement is well illustrated by their use of non-Christian sources. Clement devoted page after page to lengthy citations from Greek poetry[23] beginning with Hesiod. Origen by contrast displays practically no familiarity with the literature of Greece, except in *Against Celsus* where, not unlike Augustine in the *City of God*, he displays considerable knowledge of Greek philosophy but none at all of non-philosophical Greek literature. Interestingly, as we shall see, on several occasions he quotes passages from the works of the second century AD Pythagorean philosopher, Numenius of Apamea, whose writings, above all his treatise *On the Good*, exercised an even greater influence on Eusebius of Caesarea, who cites him very frequently in book xi of his *Preparation for the Gospel*. It is also due to Eusebius in his *Ecclesiastical History* VI, xix that we learn that Origen was conversant with the writings of Numenius – a statement derived from Porphyry.[24]

Origen's characteristic contribution is to be seen against a background of the three movements of his time against which he articulated his own position. First, he is always 'the anti-gnostic gnostic', the defender of the place both of freedom and the use of

---

[23]Clement, *Miscellanies, 5 & 6*.
[24]Porphyry, *Against the Christians* in 15 books circa 290 AD destroyed in 448 by imperial decree. The fragments were collected by Harnack. Origen acknowledges his debt to Numenius at *Contra Celsum*, 4, 51 and 5, 38.

the mind in Christianity against the determinism of both Valentinus and Basilides and the stress they laid on the utter mysteriousness of God. Secondly, he was also the severe critic of Marcion, whose criticism of the God of the Old Testament had led him to reject the whole of the Old and large sections of the New Testament. As against Marcion, Origen always insists on the continuity of the two testaments and of the God of which they speak. For Origen the creator of the universe is identical with the Father of Jesus Christ, the Word made flesh. Finally, on at least two occasions and possible more frequently,[25] he rejected the religious approach of Montanus, which elevated ecstatic experience above the action of the enlightening effect of the spirit on the mind. Origen, therefore, can be seen, as the upholder of human freedom and intelligence, as the apostle of the continuity of the two testaments, of creation and redemption, and finally of the importance of the enlightened intelligence in religion.

It is also important to remember in trying to understand the pattern of his thought that much of his time was spent on the bible. To facilitate intelligent discussion with the Jews he produced a six column concordance of the varied versions of the Old Testament, known as the *Hexapla*. Further, in order to deal with the objections of Marcion, he produced homilies and commentaries on most of the books of the bible and developed a clearly articulated defence of the Old Testament with the help of a non-literal or allegorical interpretation of the sacred text, a practice which he defended in *De Principiis* iv, 2 appealing to the treatment accorded by Saint Paul in 1 Cor. 9.9 and 10.11 and Gal. 4.24 to certain Old Testament passages.

Origen used the Platonic tradition he had learnt from, among others, Ammonius Sakkas[26] who also taught Plotinus though, unfortunately neither he nor Origen ever actually quotes him. Indeed with the exception of Plato, the only other source mentioned is the second century Pythagorean/Platonist Numenius of Apamea, whom Origen cites with approval on four separate occasions in his *Contra Celsum*.[27] He clearly regards him as a far more sympathetic and generous Hellenist than Celsus.[28] From him he may also have

[25] Origen, *De Principiis* iii, 3: 11 and *Contra Celsum* vii, 3 & 4.
[26] Eusebius, *Ecclesiastical History* [*HE* vi.19.6].
[27] Origen, *Contra Celsum*, 1: 15; 4: 51; 5: 38 and 57.
[28] Origen, *Contra Celsum*, 1: 15.

derived in the same work the expression δευτερος θεος or second god with which to denote the divine *logos*.[29] It was Numenius, according to Eusebius, who described Plato as 'Moses speaking Attic Greek'. On other sources, he is silent and this despite the fact that Origen owed his argument for the eternal generation of the Son to Aristotle's treatment of correlatives in his *Categories*.

Origen, however, was not content to treat the Platonist tradition rhetorically after the manner of Saint Paul, Justin and Clement. In other words although those writers show a positive attitude towards Hellenism,[30] they do not attempt a structure with which to underpin and so illuminate their Christian faith. Origen by contrast does. Origen made the first systematic attempt to harmonize the tradition of the faith with the free conclusions of the human intellect. Of him Charles Bigg writes: 'The range of his activity is amazing. He is the first great scholar, the first great preacher, the first great devotional writer, the first great commentator, the first great dogmatist'.[31] Unfortunately there is little poetry in Origen and he treats the poetical books of the bible as though they were plain prose.

Before an attempt is made to assess the extent of Platonic influence on Origen, it will be helpful to explore the evidence provided by Origen's reply to the attacks on Christianity made by Celsus. Celsus' seminal work *The True Account* appeared in about 176 AD and was one of the first if not the first attempt offered by Hellenism to give a coherent outline to the beliefs and philosophy of the Greek world and so to define itself against the perceived dangers of Christianity. It rejected the attempt made by Justin and others of the Apologists to break up Hellenism into two separate elements: philosophy and religion, and then claim the first member for the gospel.

For Celsus, Christianity was dangerous – evidence that by then it was perceived as a force to be reckoned with – because it refused two factors that were thought vital for the well being of the empire, common worship and military service.[32] Worse than that, it was so new – at least Judaism was antique. Christianity was at that time hardly 150 years old. Finally, and possibly most damning of all, it

---

[29] At *Contra Celsum* v/39; vi/61; and vii/57.
[30] At times in the case of Saint Paul and more frequently in Clement.
[31] C. Bigg, *The Christian Platonists of Alexandria*, p. 151.
[32] In this charge Celsus shares much in common with Gibbon.

was a religion intended for the simple minded and not for 'cultured despisers of the gospel'.[33] So Origen cites Celsus[34] as alleging that the Christian response to accusations of anti-intellectual obscurantism was 'Don't be afraid, only believe';[35] 'All things are possible to him who believes'[36] and 'Your faith has made you well'.[37] It is not hard to see why Celsus and others made such allegations. Jesus' first disciples were drawn from fishermen and Saint Paul's words were hostile to the wisdom of this world,[38] 'which was foolishness with God'.

Had Tertullian or another writer like him been confronted with such a series of charges, above all the last, he might have conceded the point at once and agreed that verses like 'Only believe' did express an anti-intellectual fideism which was the hallmark of the gospel. Not so Origen. To begin with, he accepted the idea of κοιναι εννοιαι or 'common conceptions' to which every rational being had access. The idea was of Stoic provenance and may even have influenced Saint Paul.[39] Common conceptions are not unlike the seeds of the *logos* of which Justin speaks and were thought to explain the fact that on certain moral and religious issues then and now, people who seemed to be a long way apart in many ways were in fact in agreement. The notion makes its appearance in Philo and later in Gregory of Nyssa. In other words Origen is appealing to a commonality of basic ideas, possessed by all, and not to ideas peculiar to Christians. Alien wisdom and the Perennial Philosophy of Aldous Huxley have much in common with the gospel.

Origen goes on from here to insist that though the simple, ordinary Christian has to make do with unexamined faith, on the principle that the divine word has differing manifestations,[40] those who are possessed of intelligence should use it and learn with its aid to rid the idea of God of the misleading accretions of anthropomorphism that had crept in. In all this, Origen is hardly different from Celsus. For both authors God must be morally perfect. Origen insists, basing himself on two scriptural proof texts, Ps. 101.28 and Mal. 3.6, that

---

[33]*Contra Celsum*, 1, 9:10.
[34]Origen, *Reply*, book 1, Chapter 9.
[35]To quote Mk 5.36.
[36]Mk 9.23.
[37]Mt 9.22.
[38]Above all in the opening chapters of the *First Letter to the Corinthians*.
[39]Rom. 2.13.
[40]Origen, *Contra Celsum* 1: 16.

God is always the same.[41] He must also possess the four qualities of power, wisdom, goodness and justice and not simply take refuge in the saying of Jesus 'God can do everything'[42] when pressed by a difficulty. This point is emphasized. He writes: 'In our opinion God is able to do everything that he can do, without abandoning his position as God, and as good and as wise'.[43] Very similar strategies are adopted by Gregory of Nyssa in the prologue to his *Catechetical Oration*. The idea of what is fitting for God to do and be dominates the discussion in both writers. Both also depend on the use of common notions, κοιναι εννοιαι.[44] By this phrase they mean moral and religious ideas common to all.

God must, above all, be free of the vice of anger. Origen discusses the matter at some length in *Contra Celsum* 4: 72. In this, Origen follows in the footsteps of the second century Apologists, for whom αοργησια was a virtue as it had been, as we have seen, for Clement of Rome.[45] Origen's treatment of the subject in *On First Principles* ii, 4: 4 in which he refers to his exegesis of Ps. 2.5: 'Then he will speak to them in his anger, and in his wrath he will disturb them'. None of the passages alleged by Marcion are to be taken literally. 'All demand a spiritual interpretation'.

The basic problems raised by the so called 'Platonism' of Origen are two in number: First, what variety of Platonism are we dealing with? And secondly, and more importantly, to what extent, if at all, the structures of Platonism took the place of the religion of the bible and the rule of faith in his writings? Above all, did Origen's desire to establish the philosophical credibility of the gospel lead him to produce a concept of God from which all elements of freedom had been systematically eradicated, so that he is as it were constricted by our ideas of him?

On the first point, it must not be thought that second century Platonism was homogeneous. In addition to the presupposition that dominates the writings of both Alcinous and Apuleius, that a satisfactory amalgam of Plato and Aristotle may be created, we find also the position of Atticus. So Merlan writes:

---

[41]Origen, *Contra Celsum* 1: 21.
[42]Mt. 19: 26.
[43]Origen, *Contra Celsum* 3: 70.
[44]Origen, *Against Celsus* 1: 4 and Gregory, *Catechetical Oration* 5.
[45]Clement of Rome, *Letter to the Corinthians*, Section 19.

Albinus (=Alcinous) and Apuleius represent an almost complete synthesis of Plato with Aristotle. Atticus represents the other extreme. He vigorously objects to Platonists who find Aristotelian doctrines helpful to Platonism'.[46]

Almost all our knowledge of Atticus comes from books xi and xv of the *Praeparatio Evangelica* of Eusebius, whereas of Alcinous we hear nothing. Our knowledge of his *Handbook of Platonism* derives from the library of Arethas in the tenth century. Interestingly several of the passages cited insist on the harmony of Plato and the Hebrew Scriptures and find the ideas of Aristotle particularly defective both in his reduced view of divine providence and his treatment of the soul as merely the entelechy or form of the body without the hope of a future immortality, a view quite unlike that of Plato that we find in the *Phaedo* and *Meno*. Interestingly we find a similar criticism of Aristotle also in Tatian. This suspicion of Aristotle persisted till the sixth century. Even John Philoponus (c.490–c.570), though deeply influenced by Aristotle, rejected his science.

Origen was clearly aware of the possibility of an accusation of plagiarism. He defends the gospel against the charge of inferiority to or plagiarism from Plato.[47] He points out in so doing that although Plato, the son of Ariston, was correct in his *Seventh Letter* in identifying the absolute first good with God and so evidenced the truth of Saint Paul's words at Rom. 1.21, the opening words of his *Republic* make it clear that he persisted in his idolatry. In other words, it was Plato's fundamental inconsistency that was at fault, not his actual delineation of the characteristics of the Supreme Being.

The nature of the actual dependence of Origen upon philosophy is further raised by the question about the meaning of αρχαι (archai) or principles in the title of *De principiis*. The tension referred to illustrates the fundamental ambiguity for the interpreter in assessing Origen's general approach and the distinctive character of his theology. Are the principles basically the truths contained in the bible and the rule of faith or are they the primal philosophical ideas on which his system is thought to depend?

---

[46]Merlan, *The Cambridge History of Later Greek and Early Mediaeval Philosophy* (Cambridge University Press, 1967), p. 73.
[47]Origen, *Contra Celsum* vi: 3.

Some German commentators[48] think that the two aspects are inseparable. Others, like Madame Harl and Professor Wiles, see in the title an affirmation of the radically Christian character of the enterprise. Others again argue that the principles in Alcinous' *Handbook* are those of philosophy.[49] There is much to be said in favour of this position. We find Alcinous speaking of the 'first principles' which are for him matter, the forms and God.[50] We find another second century Platonist, Apuleius of Madaura naming the '*tria initia*' which are precisely the same as those of his Greek counterpart God, matter and the forms.[51] The basic dependence on Plato's *Timaeus* is clear.

Origen himself is guarded in his approach to philosophy as his *Homilies on Joshua* 7: 7 well illustrate. There he is discussing the sin of Achor who had tried, unsuccessfully, to hide the treasures he had stolen from Jericho and was stoned to death for his pains.[52] Origen uses the incident as an opportunity to attack the 'perverse teachings of the philosophers' above all when expressed in elegant diction. He then illustrates his position by arguing that the major heretics, Valentinus, Basilides and Marcion, were over influenced by the eloquence of philosophy. This is an unintentionally ironic observation when we recall that Origen himself was to be bracketed with the Gnostics and other heretics for his adhesion to philosophy. Here it looks as if Origen were committing himself to Harnack's view that Gnosticism represents an 'acute Hellenization of Christianity'.[53]

As was mentioned above, one of the central problems in Origen is the extent to which his system allows for any change in God. His stress on the divine immutability in both his scriptural and philosophic writings makes it hard for him to admit of any change at all. What *looks* like change in God is really a change in us. As we shall see in his treatment of the Incarnation, the problem of admitting change in God is not easily side-stepped. Any change in God even for the purpose of performing a miracle implies some

---

[48]For example Lothar Lies, *Origenes' peri archon*, p. 8.
[49]As in the recent 1985 edition: Alcinous, *Handbook*, Gorgemanns and Karpp (eds), (1985), p. 10.
[50]Alcinous, *Handbook*, at the beginning of Chapter 8.
[51]Apuleius of Madaura, *De Platone et eius dogmate*, i: 5.
[52]Josh. 7.19-26.
[53]Harnack, *History of Doctrine*, vol. 1.

form of imperfection both in God himself and in the universe for which he is ultimately responsible. All change is either for the better or the worse. Both are incompatible with the thought of God as perfect in every way.

Origen's treatment of the wrath of God, as we have seen, is a case in point. In Rom. 1.18, in his *Commentary* on Rom. 1.16 and especially where he searches for the *spiritualis intellectus 'sicut intelligere de Deo dignum est'*,[54] Origen effectively rules out the possibility of change. In the former passage, he interprets anger to mean that power that is used by those who punish malefactors to bring them to a better frame of mind, all punishment being for Origen corrective or, as in Plato's *Gorgias*, medicinal. In other words anger is a way of describing the way God improves the human race through his chosen agents. It has nothing whatever to do with an expression of strong emotion.

Are we here and in other passages in the presence of the undue influence of philosophy on the gospel? While remarking on the divisive character of Origen,[55] Chadwick does not make his own position clear. Henri Crouzel labels Origen's approach 'research' rather than 'systematic',[56] and finds in him a more orthodox writer. More recently, Mark Edwards finds in Origen a writer who removed from the Platonist tradition those elements which could not be incorporated within the framework of the rule of faith, elements such as eternal creation, the fall of souls and universal salvation.[57] Even so, despite this benign approach is it possible to say that Origen's position is unplatonic? The accusation of the over influence of Platonism was clear from earliest days, as we shall see.

The question is peculiarly acute when we come to the discussion of Origen's 'Subordinationism'. Are Alcinous and Numenius and Ammonius Sakkas responsible for his views – the last named being apparently Origen's master?[58] Origen's own account of the nature of the first two principles and of their relationship to each other appears in the first book of *On First Principles* where Origen offers us an account of what he means by God the Father: He is

---

[54]Origen, *On First Principles* 2, 4: 4.
[55]H. Chadwick, *Early Christian Thought and the Classical Tradition*, p. 95.
[56]H. Crouzel, *Origene et la philosophie*, Paris, 1963, p. 69.
[57]M. Edwards, *Origen against Plato*.
[58]If Eusebius reporting of Porphyry at *HE* vi, xix, 7 is to be trusted.

an incorporeal, simple, intellectual nature; a monad or henad – language derived ultimately from the *Pythagoras*, though not to be found in Numenius. This same God is mind and the source of all intellectual being.

The juxtaposition of mental characteristics derived from Aristotle, and verbal ones, monad, dyad and the rest, from Pythagoreanism is striking. So too is the conjunction of mind and simplicity, for how can a mental being be also thought of as simple? Thought implies a distinction of subject and object; absolute simplicity rules it out. Though beyond the reach of the bodily senses, this same God can be perceived by the senses of the soul, or spiritual senses.[59] He is also morally perfect, above all just and good.[60]

From this first Father God comes by a process of eternal generation, the Son, the divine Word and Wisdom. The argument deployed by Origen[61] to prove this point is derived from Aristotle's Categories and rests on the assumption that correlatives must coexist. Christians admit that if God is both eternal and therefore changeless on the one hand and Father on the other, this leads necessarily to the conclusion that the Son also must exist eternally.

Unfortunately for Origen his argument took him too far. He proved too much. If God is not only eternally Father but also does not become creator or begin to create, God is eternally creator, with him there is no time, what he is he is eternally. It would appear to follow from this premise that creation, at least spiritual creation is also eternal. This conclusion is clearly drawn when he writes that there was never a moment in which God was not the providential creator and benefactor of the universe.[62] Such logic appears to lead straight to the condemned doctrine of eternal creation.

This same Word or Son is the second God and is a reality or substance quite distinct from his Father. This insistence derives from a desire to avoid any suggestion of Modalism. But further than that, the second God lacks the absolute simplicity which is one of the distinguishing features of the primary God. In his discussion of the nature of the Son/Word,[63] Origen discusses the various predicates

---

[59] Origen, *De Principiis* I, 1: 9 and Origen, *Contra Celsum* 1, 48.
[60] Origen, ii, 5: 1.
[61] Origen, *On First Principles* 1, 2: 2 and 1, 2: 10.
[62] Origen, *On First Principles* 1, 4: 3.
[63] Origen, *On First Principles* 1, 2.

of the Son and later in the same text he writes about the '*multi intellectus de Christo*'[64] – a clear reference to the many aspects or επινοιαι (*epinoiai*) discernible in Christ. So too the *Commentary on John* which he probably composed before his departure from Alexandria in 231, Origen indicates the point very clearly. He writes that while God (with an article) is in all respects both one and simple, our Saviour, God (without an article) is multiple and is made up of a number of aspects or επινοιαι (*epinoiai*) like light, resurrection, propitiation, word and wisdom, all expressions derived from the New Testament, which are applied to the second person of the Trinity but not to the Father.[65]

Even more is inferred from the plural character of the Son, which serves not only to distinguish him from the Father, but also to subordinate him to the Father, it being a principle of Greek philosophy that simplicity is superior to complexity. Even so it must be admitted it is not altogether clear why the aspects of the Son should be treated as plurals, while the justice, power, wisdom and goodness of the Father are not thought of as aspects of God. In any event, it does seem to be true that despite his doctrine of the eternal generation of the Son from the Father, Origen is indebted to his Platonism for the principle which underlies the structuring of his theology that simplicity is in every way prior to plurality.

Origen on the Incarnation

It is when Origen comes to addressing the problem of the Incarnation that he finds himself peculiarly challenged. For how was it possible for the universally provident and present divine Word of God to be totally and uniquely present in a particular human being, Jesus of Nazareth? Origen evolves two separate strategies with which to face this problem. In the earlier of these he asks how it was possible for the one 'through whom all things visible and invisible were made' should have appeared in the narrow confines of a particular person and place.[66] Could the particularity of the Incarnation be made philosophically acceptable? His reply entails an appeal to the

---

[64] Origen, *On First Principles* 2, 7: 3.
[65] Origen, *Commentary on John* 1, 20: 119.
[66] Origen, *On First Principles* 2, 2: 3–6, especially 2, 6:2.

differing responses offered by human beings to the same reality. Some respond warmly, others less so. Some respond so passionately that they become one with the object of their admiration and love. Such Origen says was the case with the human created soul of Jesus. It was so enamoured with the divine Word that it became one with it, even as iron becomes one with fire in which it is placed.[67] This language owes much to the Stoic theory of mixture. So the divine takes over the human soul of Christ without destroying it, as does the fire without destroying the iron. In this model the mystical ascent makes Christ the first but not the only one to arrive at the unison here described. In his discussion of the nature of the union between the human soul and the divine *Logos*, Origen appeals[68] to a verse from Saint Paul which becomes a powerful force at the heart of his spirituality: 'He that is joined to the Lord is one spirit with him'.[69]

The later treatment of the same problem occurs at the opening of the fourth book of his *Against Celsus*. Origen again faces the same sort of problem: If the Word of God is both omnipresent and omniscient, how and why could or should he come down to our level? What could be gained by it? Surely the divine Word is not in need of further information. Origen's reply is that the descent is simply a way of saying that to this universal condescension of the Word who is always descending there are varied categories of response. The best response of all was that made by Jesus – hence his distinctive character.

In his treatment of Celsus' objections to the incarnation, Origen insists that it is not God the Word who undergoes a change or begins to do things, he is always the same and omnipresent, it is we that change.[70] He seems to assimilate the Incarnation therefore both to prophecy and holiness – a move which seems to deprive the Incarnation of its unique character. In so dealing with 'the scandal of particularity', does Origen differ importantly from Celsus' rejection of the possibility of novelty in a fixed system?

Apart from turning the Christian message into a form of meritocracy, it is not at all clear on this model or on its predecessor

---

[67] Origen, *On First Principles*, 2, 6: 6.
[68] Origen, *On First Principles* 2, 6: 3.
[69] 1 Cor. 6.17.
[70] Origen, *Against Celsus*, 4, 7–8.

how Origen protects the crucial point of the gospel, namely the unique character of the Incarnation, if it is at least in principle possible for every rational being to achieve that degree of moral and spiritual maturity which predisposes and enables union with the Word. It is hard to resist the conclusion that both in his grading of the persons of the Trinity and in his account of the person of Christ, Origen is using ideas which despite their scriptural dress depend on philosophy. Incarnation, which appeared to suggest that at a particular moment in time the eternal, changeless Word of God began to be something he had not previously been becomes, in Origen's treatment, a way of describing the way the human soul can relate to God. On this point, Chadwick writes: 'In Celsus's view the root of the matter lies in the Biblical doctrine of God'.[71] Nothing can be at the same time new and true. For Origen, the intense relationship of Christ's human soul to the divine Word was not a new event, but one which went back to the eternal relationship of the human soul of Christ to the divine Word of God. It was certainly not new.

It is instructive to contrast Origen's treatment of the Incarnation with that of Athanasius. Athanasius was well aware of the difficulties inherent in the whole doctrine of the Incarnation. He lays them out in Section 8 of his own treatise *On the Incarnation*. In a later work, *Against the Arians*, he writes, perhaps with Origen's position in mind, that when the Word became flesh, it was not as though Christ were a saint or a prophet. 'He [that is the divine Word] became man, He did not come into a man . . . It is essential to grasp this point'.[72] Origen's Christ is in danger of being reduced to the condition of saint or prophet. He is more than that. The incarnation is a unique moment in time. It is particular and cannot be repeated.

Origen on generation and creation out of nothing

We can now turn to Origen's treatment of the doctrine of creation and see how far if at all he distinguishes it from the doctrine of the eternal generation of the Son. By the time the creed of Nicaea

---

[71]H. Chadwick, *Early Christianity and the Classical Tradition*, p. 25.
[72]Athanasius, *Against the Arians*, 3: 30.

of 325 came to be formulated, the distinction clearly was asserted with the words 'begotten not made'. The journey to this clarity took some time.

The emergence of the idea of Creation out of nothing[73] took place over a period of time and in response to certain impulses. Three motives can be discerned for the emergence of an idea that is largely, if not entirely, missing from the bible except perhaps in Genesis 1 and 2 *Macc.* 7.23. In the latter passage, the mother of the Maccabees addresses her sons with the following stirring words: 'Therefore the creator of the world who shaped the beginning of humankind and devised the origin of all things'. The idea plays no part in any of the great Greek philosophers. The first clear assertion comes in a mid second century Christian work *The Shepherd of Hermas Mandate 1*, a text cited by Irenaeus;[74] Origen[75] and Athanasius.[76] The passage reads as follows: 'First of all believe that God is one, who created and ordered all things making them to exist out of nothing'.

Three motives have been proposed for the development of this teaching. First, in Greek philosophy itself there was a growing awareness of the importance of undiminished source, especially an insistence on the power of God and his independence of the matter he fashions. This by itself is an advance upon the account of creation offered by Plato in the *Timaeus*, where matter and the ideas are coeternal. In Plotinus all comes from the One by a process of fall away or emanation for which he offers at *Ennead* 5, 1: 1 no clear explanation. He also rejects, at *Ennead* 3, 2: 1, an artisan view of creation. So Basilides, despite his view of emanation does insist that all comes from the ultimate God. Although the Irenaean account of Basilides' teaching[77] makes no reference to creation out of nothing, Hippolytus in his *Philosophumena* does make such an assertion.

Secondly, there was a growing anti-Gnosticism, which insisted that God made all with his own hands and further that matter was not the result of sin or incapacity. This is especially clear in Irenaeus *Demonstration* 4 'the origin of all is God' and also in the strong

---

[73]Cf. G. May, *Schopfung aus dem Nichts* (Berlin, 1978).
[74]Irenaeus, *Demonstration*, 4.
[75]Origen, *De Principiis* 1, 3: 3.
[76]Athanasius, *On the Incarnation*, 3.
[77]*In Adversus Haereses* I, 24.

monotheism of Theophilus *ad Autolycum* 1, 4. Both writings come from the end of the second century.

Thirdly, a strong need was felt to articulate a clear distinction between the generation of the Word and the creation of the world which is clearly expressed in the creed of 325 and in Athanasius *Against the Arians* 2.2, and much less clearly in either Origen or Arius neither of whom makes a clear distinction as we shall see between the divine Son and the created order.

Origen was in something of a difficulty on this issue. He clearly wishes to establish a difference between the Son and creation, yet how could he do this in the face of his view that God's eternity could not easily accommodate any new decisions. As he argues, God does not begin to be omnipotent or to create any more than he began to be Father.[78] That being the case, some doctrine of eternal creation seems to follow. Indeed, Origen's insistence on the divine eternity presented him with difficulties both in dealing with the place of petitionary prayer in a Christian life and with the particularity of the Incarnation.

It is only fair to Origen to point out that he does make a distinction between spiritual and material creation, the former is from eternity, the latter not so owing its distinct existence to the inability of the former to remain in the condition in which it first came to be, as the spiritual church before the casting down of the material world to make a place of improvement for the fallen spirits. Origen's views on the pre-existent church and the fall of souls occurs in several places in his writings, notably at *On First Principles* 3, 5: 4, echoing Eph. 1.4 owes much to a similar account of the fall of souls described by Plato in his dialogue the *Phaedrus*, where Plato offers an account 'of the other souls' and of the way in which after a lapse of ten thousand years they acquire once more the wings that were lost.[79]

The Platonic identification of *protologia* and *eschatologia* is mirrored in Origen's own account of the progress of the soul back to its beginning. Here too we are faced with a difficulty. How can Origen reconcile the apparent necessity of the identity of end and beginning with his stress on the need for meritocracy and the need to safeguard liberty?

---

[78] Origen, *On First Principles*, 1, 2: 10.
[79] Plato, *Phaedrus*, 248.

Attitudes to Origen in later Christian antiquity

The latter history of the varied attitudes to Origen is not without interest, and helps to highlight the highly ambiguous character of his contribution to the history of theology. He was criticized by Methodius of Olympus (died c.311) in a work entitled *On the Resurrection* for his supposed denial of the resurrection of the body. In it, Methodius insists against Origen on the identity of the resurrection body with that borne in this life. Eustathius of Antioch, bishop from 324 till his expulsion by Constantine sometime between 327 and 330, attacked Origen's allegorical methods in his treatise *On the Witch of Endor*.

Defences of the master were prepared by his pupils, notably by Gregory Thaumaturgos on his departure from Caesarea in about 240 for Cappadocia. It was he who converted Macrina, the grandmother of Basil and Gregory of Nyssa, and through this channel some at any rate of the characteristic attitudes of Origen found their way into Cappadocian theology. Half a century later Pamphilus, with his five volume *Apologia Origenis* written sometime before 310, tried to rescue Origen, whom he can never have known, from charges touching on his Trinitarian and Incarnational faith. It is here that we find Origen replying to various slurs on his orthodoxy, which were doubtless already current. According to Pamphilus, Origen actually used the controversial coinage '*homoousios*' in his now lost *Commentary on the Letter to the Hebrews*.[80] Also it is possible to detect a certain apologetic tone in the extensive information provided by Eusebius in book 6 of his *History*, in which he fails to mention critics like Methodius. This is hardly surprising once we recall that Eusebius was a disciple of the same Pamphilus who had defended Origen.

On the one hand his subsequent influence upon the Cappadocians[81] seen in the *Philocalia* produced by Basil and Gregory of Nazianzus in 358 with the intention of arguing from Origen's text, above all in *De Principiis*, for the rational character of the inspired text of scripture and for the importance of the freedom of the will

---

[80][MPG xvii.580 C].
[81]Gregory of Nazianzus, *Letter* 115.

for the nature of the relationship of scripture and reason Gregory of Nyssa cites him by name on two occasions and was more indebted to him above all in the area of spirituality than were either his brother, Basil or their mutual friend, Gregory of Nazianzus. This was largely positive, though not often overtly affirmed. Although Origen's influence is everywhere present in Basil's *On the Holy Spirit*, he mentions him specifically by name only once at Section 73. It is possible that his awareness of the hostility felt and expressed towards Origen by Epiphanius only a year before his *On the Holy Spirit*, which is 375, made him unwilling to annex too much authority to his writings.

On the other hand Cappadocian sympathy for Origen was severely qualified by further attacks on him, which began to proliferate as the fourth century drew to a close. On the latter history of the controversy surrounding Origen at the end of the fourth century Elizabeth Clark's *The Origenist Controversy*[82] should be consulted. As early as 374 Epiphanius, the heresy hunting bishop of Salamis from 367 to 403, clearly believed that Origen's views were very dangerous to orthodox Christianity. His immense attack on Origen[83] makes this clear, well before Jerome's 'conversion'. It ends with the claim that Origen had been blinded by Greek learning, with the following censure: 'So you too Origen were mentally blinded by the aforesaid education of the Greeks and vomited your poison on those who were persuaded by you'.[84] The poisonous nature of the perceived views of Origen could hardly be more forcibly expressed. For Epiphanius Origen was infected by Hellenism which was the source and was therefore cause of Arianism.[85]

In 393 (or 396), some 160 years after Origen's death, Jerome was converted from his erstwhile favourable attitude to Origen to one of acute hostility. Apparently the publication by Rufinus of his translation of the first two books of Origen's *De Principiis* in 398 provoked him even further. In much of his critique, he was in a large measure dependent upon Epiphanius. Part of his motive seems to have been the fear that his earlier admiration for Origen, above all manifest in his use of Origen's commentaries on the Pauline epistles

---

[82]E. Clark, *The Origenist Controversy,* (Princeton, 1993).
[83]Epiphanius, *Panarion* 64 [=MPG 41 1068-1200].
[84]Epiphanius, 64, 73.
[85]Epiphanius, *Panarion* 64, 4.

above all *Philemon*, *Galatians*, *Ephesians* and *Titus* might discredit him with such powerful figures as Epiphanius and Theophilus the Pope of Alexandria. It is instructive to compare Jerome's somewhat erratic attitude to Origen with the more balanced perspective of Augustine. In the course of his ill fated correspondence with Jerome in letter 40, he speaks of making a distinction between those things that are true and right in him that we should praise, and his wrong views that we should condemn.

The whole depressing story of the conflict between Theophilus and John Chrysostom, which was immediately connected with the persecution by the former of the Origenist monks of Egypt, is related in detail both by Elizabeth Clark and more recently by J. N. D. Kelly.[86] The final blow fell in 543 at the synod in the anathemata against Origen, which were reaffirmed at the Second Council of Constantinople itself ten years later. At the earlier synod assembled under the Patriarch Menas, nine anathemata were pronounced against Origen for his supposed support of the doctrines of the pre-existence of the soul [1], the spherical nature of the resurrection body [5], the finite nature of God [8] and the doctrine of universal salvation [9].

Subsequent writers on Origen like Mark Edwards, Henri Crouzel and Henry Chadwick are inclined to dismiss these condemnations as mischievous. Even so, propositions 1, 8 and 9 are clear inferences from the system proposed by Origen and as it were, make sense of it. It is perhaps only fair to note that the idea of the divine infinity, so much used by Gregory of Nyssa, is a much less obvious 'doctrine' than is sometimes supposed. It seems to have made its first clear appearance in Christian theology in the writings of the Gnostic Valentinus as recorded for us by Irenaeus.[87] On the other hand, the doctrine of universal salvation or *apokatastasis* is also to be found in Gregory of Nyssa, a fact which although it caused the Eastern church some embarrassment, never issued in his posthumous excommunication.

---

[86] J. N. D. Kelly, *Golden Mouth*, chs 14–16.
[87] Irenaeus, *Against the Heresies*, 1, 17 (book I, Chapter 17).

Conclusion

Despite or perhaps because of his brilliance Origen is never an easy figure to evaluate. Henry Chadwick quotes a passage from Gennadius II Patriarch of Constantinople under the Turks in the fifteenth century. It runs as follows:

> The Western writers say, "Where Origen is good, no one is better, where he is bad no one is worse." Our Asian divines say on the other hand that "Origen is the whetstone of us all", but on the other hand, that "he is the fount of foul doctrines".[88]

The difficulty with assessing Origen's attitude or rather debt to philosophy lies precisely here. To what extent is it fair to blame philosophy for the errors into which he fell? For example, if it is assumed that Origen owed his doctrine of the immortality of the soul and of the eternal generation of the Son to philosophy, is it fair to blame philosophy for the apparent adoption by Origen of the fall of souls into bodies because of prenatal sin or the eternity of the spiritual world as well as that of the eternal Son? He would not cease to be a debtor to philosophy if he had failed to draw some of the conclusions.

---

[88]H. Chadwick, *Early Christian Thought and the Classical Tradition*, Chapter 4 (at the beginning of the chapter).

4

The influence of philosophy on the language and thought of the councils

The purpose of this chapter, unlike that of Chapters 3 and 5, is less to look at the way individual Christian writers related to the philosophy of their age than to explore the ideas and language that were deployed in the definition of Christian doctrine between Nicaea (325) and Chalcedon (451). Although writers of the stature of Origen, Gregory of Nyssa and Augustine were all in their different ways concerned to explore the nature of God, his unity and threefoldness, and the nature of Christ, their resultant theology did not always or immediately command the assent of all the church. Conciliar decisions carried more authority and the question before us is about the extent to which these pronouncements were influenced by the philosophy of their day. There is also a supplementary question. It was a mark of those who came to be thought of as orthodox to stigmatize the writings of their opponents as tainted by philosophy and therefore dangerous and misleading. To what extent is this true? Were Arius, Eunomius and Nestorius any more indebted to the philosophy of their day than were their critics, Athanasius, Basil and Cyril of Alexandria?

The early church believed in what may seem to us like contradictory positions. On the one hand, they believed in the value of language in expressing the nature both of God and Christ. In this conviction they were true Greeks. On the other hand they were also aware of the limitations of language, above all of its ultimate frailty in the face of the divine mystery. Language was vital. God had revealed himself in time through language and in history. Yet despite that it could only go so far, especially alongside the conviction that God was indeed beyond the grasp of human intelligence and language.

The vision and 'conversion' of Constantine and his subsequent victory at the battle of the Milvian Bridge in 312 ushered in a new era for the Christian church. She began to experience peace and patronage, whereas prior to that she had been subject to intermittent bouts of persecution under Decius in 250, under Valerian in 258 and most recently under Diocletian in 305. But imperial patronage, the ability to use the imperial postal service and the freedom from vexatious interference exacted its own tribute.

The emperor and his successors assumed that they were in the footsteps of Augustus. They continued to use the title *pontifex maximus* until Gratian dropped it at the insistence of Ambrose in 382. For all of them, a healthy civil society was intimately connected with a united religious one. In this too Constantine and his sons assumed, as had Diocletian, that political health was intimately linked to religious uniformity. The state religion was now effectively Christian and Constantine realized that it was not in his interest to permit the existence of dissident Christian groups, even as his immediate predecessor, Diocletian had been unwilling to tolerate religious pluralism. According to Eusebius,[1] he also thought of himself, to the surprise of the other clergy present, as 'bishop of those outside the church'.

For Constantine, therefore, divisions among Christians were not simply private affairs that he could afford to ignore. Rather were they perceived as a threat to the unity and health of his empire. Two particular divisions among Christians arrested the attention of the emperor, Donatism – a product of the recent persecution of Diocletian, with its ideal of a pure church – and Arianism. The former of these two threats was addressed, but not satisfactorily resolved,

---

[1] Eusebius, *Life of Constantine*, iv, 24.

in 314 at the Council of Arles not long after his conversion and victory at the battle of the Milvian Bridge. Arianism was, it would appear, a slightly later development, datable to about 318. In both of these cases, it was as much the desire for the peace and unity of the church as much as concern with the underlying dogmatic issue that led Constantine to summon a council at Antioch and shortly after that, in the same year, the First Ecumenical Council at Nicaea (modern Isnik) in May 325.

Arius and Arianism

The first person to be solemnly condemned for heresy by a council of the whole church, east and west, was Arius. It would however be wrong to infer from this that deviations from some sort of dogmatic norm were unknown before that date. Initially, the word heresy had no unwelcome sense, and meant simply a school of thought or an opinion. It had acquired a negative sense as early as the beginning of the second century in a letter written by Ignatius of Antioch to the church at Tralles, and seems to refer to the dangers of Docetism, that is of denying the real human nature of Jesus. The views of the Gnostics in the second century and of Paul of Samosata in the third had also been censured, the latter in two councils held in Antioch in 264 and 268, though these assemblies never acquired the authority of the later ecumenical councils, largely because they lacked imperial backing and summons. Indeed it would be hard to imagine the pagan emperors showing the slightest interest in inner church disputes, which they would have doubtless regarded with the same contempt as did a later rationalist like Edward Gibbon.

Unfortunately for a fair assessment of Arius' views, he is not easily accessible to us owing to the fragile and tendentious nature of the sources that preserve his teaching. Our principal knowledge of the views of Arius stems from the treatise of Athanasius entitled *On the Synods*. Chapters 15 and 16 of this work give us, respectively, extracts from Arius' verse poem entitled *Thalia*, and the *Letter of Arius to Alexander, Bishop (or Pope) of Alexandria*. What then were the central tenets of Arius? Assuming as we must that in the *Letter of Arius to his Bishop in Alexandria, Alexander* gives an accurate enough account of his views, we can sum them up as follows.

In this letter written in about 320 AD, Arius writes:

Our faith from our forefathers, which we have learnt from thee, Blessed Pope, is this: We acknowledge One God, alone unbegotten, alone everlasting (*Psalm* 102, (101): 26), alone true (*John* 17: 3), alone having immortality (1 Timothy 6: 16), alone wise (*Romans* 16: 27), alone good (*Mark* 10: 18), alone sovereign; judge, governor, administrator of all, unalterable and unchangeable, the just and good God of Law and prophets and New Testament; who begat an only begotten Son before eternal times . . . and made him to subsist at his own will . . . perfect creature of God, but not as one of the creatures. . .'.

He opens with an assertion of the traditional, received nature of his views. He goes on to insist upon the absolute aloneness of God, whom he hardly ever refers to as Father. The evidence upon which this scheme rests is entirely biblical, as the texts adduced indicate. This absolute deity, by an act of will then produces an offspring – the Son. This same Son seems not to be coeternal with the Father, although Arius tries to purchase for the Son an intermediate or go-between condition or status between the eternity of God and the temporal character of creatures by saying of him: 'There was when he was not'. There are, therefore, three basic ideas upon which the system of Arius rests: first, the divine aloneness; secondly, the divine will; and thirdly, the in-between status of the Son.

On the one hand the 'evidence' adduced by Arius is entirely drawn from the Old and New Testament as the quotations illustrate. It is also worth noting that, on the whole, Arius avoids applying the word Father to God and insists on relating the Son to the first God by will. In this aspect also, Arius expresses a biblical vision. Will is mentioned as the agent of production on two occasions in his *Letter* and on three in his *Thalia*.

Standing as he does in the Alexandrian tradition, Arius' departure from certain basic elements of that structure is remarkable. The stress on the sovereign freedom of God stands in marked contrast to the argument used by Origen in *On First Principles* 1, 2: 2, which argues on the basis of the principle of correlatives for the eternal generation of the Son – a conclusion to which Origen is led by his very New Testament insistence on the idea of God as essentially and eternally Father. This leads him to argue for, and to insist upon, his characteristic teaching of the eternal generation of the Son.

Plotinus also, in his effort to derive the All from the One, is opposed to the use of anything like artisan or 'free language' with which to do so. For him there is not, nor can there be, any uncertainty. Indeed at the opening of *Ennead* 3, he appears to have Christians in mind, when he writes that both foresight and reasoning in God are out of place.[2] In another *Ennead* entitled 'On Free Will and the Will of the One', Plotinus denies the possibility of any form of contingency or chance in the One. He writes that 'freedom is not an attribute of the First. It is as a form of self determination that freedom must be understood, but not as moving towards any other'.[3] There seems very little in common between this very refined notion of freedom and the idea of the will as expressed in the letter of Arius.

If we assume that the extracts offer an accurate account of what Arius actually wrote, the questions they raise as to the basic thrust of Arius are already clear. Not only the standard question 'Was Arius an Arian?' but also supposing the real Arius to be presented in these short extracts, what is the basic thrust of his teaching? Was his theology the child of philosophy, and as Stead[4] and Williams[5] have urged, a form of what is termed middle Platonism? Williams argues that Arius was influenced by Anatolius, a lapsed Aristotelian, who subsequently became Bishop of Laodicea. Eusebius writes of him that 'for his learning and secular education and philosophy, he had attained the first place among his illustrious contemporaries'.[6] Unfortunately we know nothing of his actual views, so Williams may be correct but does not really illuminate.[7]

Or was he determined to keep alive a biblical faith, stressing the scriptural doctrine of the aloneness and absolute freedom of God? Or was he, as Gregg and Groh argue in *The Dynamics of Salvation*,[8] an adoptionist who, in his desire to make Christ a model for us and for our salvation, felt the need to deprive him of his deity? Arius is

---

[2] Plotinus, *Enneads* 2, 1.
[3] Plotinus, *Enneads* 6, 8: 8.
[4] Stead, 'The Platonism of Arius', JTS (1964) p. 14–31.
[5] Williams, *Arius, Heresy and Tradition*, 1987.
[6] Eusebius, *Ecclesiastical History*, book 32, Chapter. 7.
[7] Williams, *Arius, Heresy and Tradition*, 1987, p. 31.
[8] Gregg and Groh, *Early Arianism: A view of salvation*, 1981.

a salvationist in their view therefore, with a particular view of how Christ saved the world, by making him really one with us and so capable of being a model. Or was he, as R. P. C. Hanson suggests in *The Christian Doctrine of God*,[9] a supporter of the '*deus passus*' view of Christ, which would be impossible to hold if you insist on the divine superiority to all feeling?[10] And does the answer to this question affect the view taken of the reply? The dilemma as to which of these options is preferable is clear from a brief look at what Arius is reported as saying. It is perhaps surprising that an author whose actual surviving remains are so slight and so questionable should provoke such fierce disagreements.

The confession of Arius at once illuminates the difficulty of categorizing him. As we have seen a good case could be made out for arguing that Arius is a biblicist. On the other hand it is clear that his structure of the divine life is not unlike that of Middle Platonism, though Alcinous would hardly have used the language of creation with which to expound his message. The Son is said by Arius to be 'perfect creature but not as one of the creatures'.[11] Slightly later he is said to be 'begotten from time before all things . . . yet is not eternal or co-eternal with God'. The obvious intention of such passages is to claim for the Son an in-between status, in between God and the created order. For later generations, he was to raise the question: 'On what side of the line separating creature and creator does the Son stand?'.

The sort of graded hierarchy implied by such language fits well into a layered universe of the type favoured by Alcinous, and other contemporary Platonists like Numenius. Alcinous insists upon the world of forms coming from the first god but inferior to him.[12] The complex postdates the simple, in origin if not in time. Somewhat later, Plotinus above all in *Ennead* 5: 1,1 offers a picture of the spiritual universe which is based on the principle of graded hierarchy, in which the absolute simplicity of the primal One is the source of Mind/Spirit, which is complex and which in its turn is the source of the third hypostasis, the World Soul.

---

[9]R. P. C. Hanson, *The Christian Doctrine of God*.
[10]See 15.2 below.
[11]Arius see *A New Eusebius* no. 284, p. 326 Edited by J. Stevenson 1957.
[12]Alcinous, *Handbook*, Section 9.

A final argument in favour of the philosophical provenance of Arian theology is Arius' use, in both the *Letter to Alexander* and in *Thalia*, of Pythagorean language with which to designate the two persons of the Trinity. The Father is the Monad and the Son the Dyad. A passage from the latter work well illustrates the mixture of language employed by Arius. 'Understand then that the Unity [i.e. Monad] was and the Duality [Dyad] was not before it existed . . . Thus the Son who was not, existed at the paternal will, is only-begotten God, and is distinct from everything else. Wisdom existed as wisdom by the will of a wise God.' This strange fusion of Pythagorean and voluntarist language raises once again the question as to whether Arius was primarily offering a philosophical account of the Father/ Son relationship, or one that rejected the language and thought world of philosophy in order to reclaim the faith for the bible.

Faced with what look like irreconcilable alternatives as lying at the root of Arian theology, is it at all possible to decide between the two? Was the primary influence on Arius the bible or philosophy? Clearly there is much to be said on both sides, and it would be no doubt possible to decide for both together. Even so, it seems better to decide for the primacy of the bible and this is for three reasons. First, the preference for will over substance language is marked in both his *Letter to Alexander* and in his *Thalia*. This preference serves to distance Arius from Origen, whose argument for the eternity of the Son assumes an Aristotelian type argument from correlatives. Again, the actual word consubstantial as a way of designating the Father/ Son relationship is explicitly rejected by Arius in both writings on the grounds that it had materialistic overtones. It is also worth noting that Arius seems strangely unwilling to speak of the divine Fatherhood. In the *Thalia* above all, God is the preferred expression for denoting the source or fountain of all things. It is at least arguable that this manifests a preference for Old Testament terminology.

Secondly, we are told by a later writer, Philostorgius (c.368– c.439), that Arius was a sort of popular evangelist, who composed his sermons in a popular metre for the benefit of his followers, that is travellers, sailors in ships and women labouring at the mill. The suggestion, therefore, is that he would hardly have managed to achieve the enviable success he clearly did if his vocabulary and thought were covertly philosophical. If this account of Arius is accepted, it will have the interesting consequence of suggesting that it is not always accurate to suggest the source of heretical opinions, or of those that were subsequently labelled as heretical, as having derived their inspiration from philosophy. Too many movements in the church have used the motto '*ad fontes*' as a definition of their programmes for us to be much surprised to find Arius doing the same.

Thirdly, a brief look at Athanasius' reply to the challenge of Arius reinforces this conclusion. His three *Orations against the Arians* are largely concerned with refuting the texts adduced by Arians from the bible, above all Prov. 8.22. This text, which reads 'The Lord created me in the beginning of his days', was used by the Arians to argue for the created and inferior character of the Son. Athanasius devotes by far the larger part of his *Second Oration*[13] to refute the Arian implications of this text. Other texts produced by the Arians were 'Therefore God has highly exalted him and bestowed on him a name that is above every name';[14] 'You love righteousness and hate wickedness; therefore God your God has anointed you with the oil of gladness'[15] and 'Having become as much superior to the angels, as the name he has obtained is more excellent that theirs'.[16]

The motive for the Arian selection of these texts is clear. They all suggest the received and non-natural character of the deity of the Son. Athanasius explains them away in a way he may have learnt from Marcellus of Ancyra that each of them referred not to the Word of God in his divine state, but to the assumed human nature. The arguments Athanasius adduces are almost entirely scriptural, though the principle they reinforce is less evidently so. However, he seems not to have detected in Arius and his followers a philosophical wolf in the clothing of a Christian sheep. In other words, he seems to have supposed that the best or indeed the only way to deal with Arius was through the vehicle of his own chosen medium – Holy Scripture.

Nicaea and the homousion

The emperor Constantine soon became aware of the disruptive potential inherent in the views of Arius and those of his close-knit followers. Though only a presbyter as even his fellow travellers

---

[13]Athanasius, *Orations against the Arians*, 2, Sections 18–82.
[14]Phil. 2.9.
[15]Ps. 45, 44.7.
[16]Heb. 1.4.

were eager to point out, Arius must have caused quite a stir in Egypt and also in Palestine. It is not easy for us to grasp quite why this was so. The Arian creed, though subsequently regarded as heretical, must have seemed orthodox enough then (and subsequently) to many people. It was certainly ambiguous and open to several interpretations. Phrases like 'a creature, but not one of the creatures' and 'he existed before times and ages, yet there was when he was not' look to us suspiciously like formulae designed to sidestep the all important question: was Christ divine or was he not?

Comprehensiveness may have certain virtues, but to the Greek mind it led to muddle or heresy or both. And for all its seeming generosity of purpose, it failed to please a large number of Christians. Its divisive character was to the fore in Constantine's efforts to bolster his political success, above all after his victory over Licinius at the Battle of Chrysopolis in 324, by a strong statement of religious unity. In his endeavour to dispose of the views and effectively of the person of Arius, the Council of Nicaea assembled at the order of the Emperor Constantine on 19 June 325. Unfortunately none of the Acts of the council survive, and we are far better informed about the twenty canons of the council than about the more influential and divisive creed.

For knowledge of the creed, we depend on three documents: the *Letter of Eusebius of Caesarea* to the people of his diocese, preserved by the fifth century ecclesiastical historian Socrates; the *Appendix to the Decrees of the Council of Nicaea* by Athanasius and *Letter 125* of Basil, dated to 373. The word consubstantial was apparently inserted into the creed at the insistence of the emperor Constantine, possibly acting under the advice of his ecclesiastical advisor Ossius, Bishop of Cordoba. Its central purpose, so it appears, was one of finding an expression that Arius could not possibly agree to. He had indeed explicitly rejected it in his Letter to Alexander.

But, if the exclusion of Arius was the main aim of the creed, had it any other purpose? Did it have a history and what did it mean? It is hard to imagine the assembled largely Greek speaking bishops making use of language which was merely introduced in order to dispose of Arius and which had no further meaning or purpose. The history of the word itself is both curious and suggestive. It had indeed been condemned along with its author, Paul of Samosata at a council held at Antioch in 268. Unfortunately, our records of this council make it unclear as to the precise sense in which consubstantial was condemned, and further attempts to make precise its meaning nearly a century later in 358 by orthodox writers of the calibre of Hilary of Poitiers in the West and Athanasius in the East did little to clear up the matter.

We need to remember that the actual word, *homousios*, was no stranger to philosophical discourse. Further, in his Categories, Aristotle outlines two distinct senses of the Greek word *ousia*. Its first sense was that of an individual entity; the second that of a class to which many items belong. If the word *homousios* was being used in the first sense, it would mean that in God there was only one reality. If in the second sense, it would mean two beings Father and Son sharing in the same divine nature. To which of these two senses did the usage of Nicaea correspond? If to the first, it would seem to lead to a form of Modalism; if to the second, did it not lead to ditheism? This was a problem that would not go away in a hurry.

Even so, whatever answer is given to this question, it seems clear that the council opted for 'substance' rather than 'will' language. In other words, although a certain degree of lack of clarity surrounds the meaning of *ousia*, leaving it perhaps deliberately unclear as to whether the strict unity or the plurality of the godhead was being asserted, there is no ambiguity surrounding the assertion that the Son belonged quite unequivocally to the divine world and not, as the thesis of Arius suggested, to some in-between condition, neither creature nor creator. The formula had the important effect, as Athanasius was not slow to point out, to make a clear distinction between Christ as the Son of God by nature and ourselves as sons of God by adoption. This vital distinction was blurred by the insistence on will language favoured by Arius. Whatever his precise intentions had his formula been successful, he would have left the church with an intolerable ambiguity, above all in answer to the exact sense in which the good man differs from his Saviour.

Whatever the rights and wrongs of the case, the Arian controversy forced the church to invest in a distinction between the language of will and that of substance. This was found necessary in order to insure that a clear distinction was made between the relation of the Son to the Father and that of the created order to its creator. The former was a necessary relationship of being or nature, the latter a freely created relation of creaturely dependence. The Son therefore *had* to exist; creatures did not. He was, to use the words of the creed, 'begotten not made'.

A further important upshot of the Arian controversy was the need to insist on the distinction between the eternal and temporal life of the Son, between what we find Gregory of Nazianzus in his *Oration* 38: 8 calling theology and economy. The Son is eternally Son enjoying a permanent relationship with the Father and the Holy Spirit. However the temporal actions of the Trinity in their respective roles of creator, redeemer and sanctifier are quite distinct from the eternal life of the Holy Trinity.

But, finally, was the actual language in any sense derived from philosophy? In the early and popular *Enneads*[17] of Plotinus, considerable parts of which were excerpted by Eusebius, we find Plotinus using the language of *homousion* with the meaning that the soul shares in the nature of the divine. 'Prudence', he writes, 'and true virtue being divine cannot coexist with what is low and mortal. It must be something divine, because it shares in divine matters because of its relationship with them and its sharing the same substance *homousion*'.[18] The suggestion therefore is that this convenient language was known at least to some of those present at Nicaea and inserted into the Creed with the dual purpose of distancing the Fathers from the views of Arius and of asserting at the same time the very close connexion enjoyed by the Son to the Father, as sharing in the same substance or nature. It is worth noting that the creeds and Fathers always speak of the consubstantiality of Son with Father and never of Father with Son.

Despite, however, the evident philosophical provenance of the central terms of the creed, in two important aspects it parts company with two important theorems of Neoplatonism. First, as Professor Dodds notes: 'the cause is superior to the effect'[19] 'This is the principle upon which the whole structure of Neoplatonism is really founded'. The assertion of the consubstantiality of the Son with the Father by contrast asserts the basic equality of the first and second principles. The fact that the Son comes from the Father does not make him therefore any less divine. He shares in the nature of his Father and is as the creed unequivocally affirms: 'Very God from very God'.

---

[17]Plotinus, *Enneads* 2, iv, 7: 10–19.
[18]Eusebius, *Preparation for the Gospel* xv: 22.
[19]Dodds, *Elements of the Theology of Proclus*, on proposition 7.

Secondly, in Neoplatonism itself with its graded hierarchy of the One, Spirit or Mind, and World Soul, and also in Origen, with whom the Father is simple, the Son diverse with many aspects, there is an unwritten assumption that what. is simple is prior and superior to what is complex. In all these systems, the first principle is always absolutely simple. In the Christianity of the creeds, however, the triune God cannot be defined as absolutely simple. He is not a monad, despite the ascription by Origen[20] of that title to God (the Father only); and the later attempt of Marcellus of Ancyra to reduce the three persons to a monad. The central tenet of the Trinity is irreconcilable with the absolute simplicity of the One. However, we need also to remember that despite these differences, the articulation of the divine into three principles – The One, Mind/Spirit and the World Soul – does bear a family resemblance to the three persons of the godhead in Christian theology. It is also worth remembering that *Ennead* 5,1 which deals expressly with the three hypostases was also excerpted by Eusebius in books 4, 5, 6, 7 and 8 of his *Preparation for the Gospel* and was probably also known to Basil. This means that this particular *Ennead* together with 4,7 and 6,9 were available to Christian writers in the middle of the fourth century, if not earlier.

All this means that despite the evident willingness of the framers of the creed to employ the language of philosophy in order to establish the absolute equality of the first and second persons of the deity, the Fathers could not adopt the two other theorems inherent in contemporary and later Platonism. The official Christian attitude to philosophy was, as it had been in Justin and Origen, both positive and at the same time selective. It shared the basic affirmation of an eternal, changeless, spiritual world with Hellenism, but it had to draw back from some of the principles on which the system rested. Christianity is not a faith that affirms the basic continuity of all things divine and human. It insists instead on the radical difference between creature and creator, between generation and creation. The Son shares in the divine nature, creatures at best reflect it, and if they are rational, aim to copy it as best they can. They copy God but unlike the Son, they do not share in his nature.

Yet it is only fair to add that even for so 'orthodox' a writer as Athanasius, who insists in *Against the Arians* that the supreme reality is a triad and not a monad, his account of the relation

---

[20] Origen, *On First Principles* 1, 1: 6.

between Father and Son is as dynamic as that of Plotinus between the One and the Spirit.[21] It is true that in Chapter 19 of the same treatise, he bases his argument on Jer. 2.13. 'They have forsaken me, the fountain of living waters'. We are not far from *Ennead* 6, 9: 5, where Plotinus speaks of the One as 'the fountain of the best things . . . but remaining undiminished in itself'.

The dynamic character of the deity is also discussed by Gregory of Nazianzus at the beginning of his third theological oration. However, and rather to our surprise, the metaphor of overflow of goodness is both likened to several passages in one of the Greek philosophers, probably Plotinus[22] though not mentioned by name, and then rejected on the grounds that flux can have no place within the nature of a being who is both perfect and changeless. 'Let us', he writes 'never look on this generation as involuntary, like some natural overflow, hard to be retained and by no means befitting our conception of the deity'. For the divine, as he tells us in Chapter 3, is above 'when'. It is interesting to find The Theologian abandoning the dynamic language of Athanasius, in preference for the will language of Arius.

Deification and Athanasius

One of the principal arguments employed by the defenders of orthodoxy in their onslaught on Arianism was that drawn from deification or divinization. For Harnack, the central idea of Athanasius' theology is that God himself entered humanity.[23] The idea that the Christian became in some way a new person through baptism and the consequent indwelling of the Holy Spirit was hardly novel. In Chapter 3 of his gospel, Saint John records a dialogue between Christ and Nicodemus in the course of which Nicodemus, to his surprise, is offered a new birth or birth from above through baptism. Romans 6 and 8 offer something very similar – resurrection and the indwelling of the Holy Spirit. By the end of the second century, we find writers as diverse as Irenaeus and Clement of Alexandria offering something very similar. Irenaeus at

---

[21]Athanasius, *Against the Arians* I, 18.
[22]Plotinus, *Enneads* 5, 2: 1.
[23]Harnack, *History of Dogma*, vol. 4.

uses Ps. 81, 82.6 'I have said you are gods and sons of the most high' in order to prove the need for the incarnation.[24] Clement on several occasions in the course of his *Address to the Greeks* praises the ideal of deification, above all through knowledge as in Chapter xi he writes of 'making men divine by heavenly doctrine'.

The precise provenance of this idea is unclear. It has antecedents in both Aristotle's *Ethics*[25] and in the end of the last *Ennead* of Plotinus. There the ideal is expressed as follows: 'This is the life of gods and of the godlike and blessed among men, liberation from the alien that besets us here, a life taking no pleasure in the things of the earth, the flight of the alone to the alone'.[26]

By the time the Arian crisis arose, the idea of the Christian vocation as somehow a closer relationship with God had become common currency in many different circles, not exclusively intellectual. Athanasius himself, who often figures as not quite philosophical if not deliberately against philosophy, employed the idea in an early work, *On the Incarnation*. Towards the end of the work he writes famously; 'He, [that is the divine Word] became man that we might become divine'.[27] Later in the course of his defence of Nicene orthodoxy, this principle is employed on several occasions to refute the Arians. His argument both at *On the Synods* 51 and *Against the Arians* 2: 70 is the same. The aim of divinization on the part of the human race depends on the prior assumption that Christ himself is fully divine. 'For he could not make us divine if he were not himself God'. In other words our own immortality and the knowledge of God, which is what Athanasius seems to mean by the idea of divinization, depend on the full deity of the divine Word.

The idea of becoming divine became fairly persistent above all with the Cappadocian Fathers and especially with Gregory of Nazianzus, though not with quite the same controversial overtones as we find in Athanasius. The actual word he uses, *theosis*, seems to have been coined by him, and he uses it extensively. In his funeral oration of his brother Caesarius, he speaks of becoming not simply divine, but actually God.[28] What he appears to mean by this is a

---

[24]Ireneus, *Against the Heresies*, 3: 20.
[25]Aristotle, *Ethics*, book x.
[26]Plotinus, *Enneads* 6, 9.
[27]Athanasius, *On the Incarnation*, Chapter 54.
[28]Gregory of Nazianzus, *Funeral Oration* 7, 23.

mixture of both *ascesis* and knowledge, somehow enabled by the indwelling presence of God. Gregory's insistence on this idea may have been occasioned by a desire to show that Christians no less than pagans offered a noble vocation in life to those who followed the gospel. But whatever the motives that underlay this use of language, it is enough to illustrate the point that Christian writers were content to use language and ideas that derived at least in part from Hellenism.

It is perhaps worthwhile noting that Gregory of Nyssa's stress on the gulf that separates God from creatures possibly makes him less insistent on the ideal of divinization than either Basil or Gregory of Nazianzus. He prefers to use the language of likeness to God or to Christ as a worthy expression of the ideal of the Christian. This he does in his second sermon on the Lord's Prayer, which is full of echoes of the passage in the *Theaetetus* of Plato, where likeness to God is presented as an ideal,[29] and links with a text from Matthew.: 'You therefore must be perfect as your heavenly father is perfect'.[30] At the opening of his *On the Life of Moses*, Gregory insists that because God himself is infinite in virtue, therefore the upward striving of the created spirit must itself imitate God in its endless upward striving. The actual vocabulary of becoming divine or God is missing. His brother Basil, evidently less aware of the potential dangers of such language, adds to the ideal of likeness to God that of becoming God.[31]

The Neo-Arians or Anomeans

Unfortunately for the church, the First Ecumenical Council, as it came to be called, left some questions open to which the answers were unclear. This was above all the case with the central word *homousios*, which, as we have seen could be interpreted to endorse a strongly unitary or even modalist understanding of the divine nature. But beyond the more strictly theological issues and the ambiguity surrounding the central word, the years following the council witnessed two further challenges. First, the removal from their sees,

---

[29]Plato, *Theaetetus*, 176a.
[30]Mt. 5.48.
[31]Basil, *On the Holy Spirit*, Chapter 9.

partly on doctrinal, partly, no doubt, on political grounds, of three of the most stalwart supporters of the Creed, Marcellus of Ancyra, Eustathius of Antioch and above all Alexander of Alexandria. For reasons which are not entirely clear critics and enemies of the Creed of Nicaea, men like the two Eusebius, of Caesarea and Nicomedia, seem to have achieved some standing as 'court bishops' both with Constantine himself and also with his son and successor Constantius. It is not at all easy to understand the triumph of the anti-Nicene school, especially if we remember that it was largely owing to the great central mass of conservative church men that the Conciliar Creed had succeeded in the first place. Secondly, the period between 325 and 360 witnessed a proliferation of at least twelve new creeds, some at Antioch, some at Sirmium and elsewhere. The exalted position the Creed of Nicaea subsequently came to enjoy had not yet arrived.

In the middle of the century the whole issue of the definition of God came to the front and was sharpened by two brilliant writers, Aetius and his pupil Eunomius. These two are sometimes called Neo-Arians or Anomoeans or Unlikers, because the upshot of their teaching was the conclusion that the Son was unlike the Father. Their views, which appeared sometime between 351 and 361, found expression in the *Syntagmatium* or *Short Treatise* of Aetius in 37 very brief propositions and the *Apology* of Eunomius in 29 short chapters. Perhaps they owed their success to their brevity. In any event, their views took Constantinople by storm and illustrate the importance that theological debates assumed in the lives of ordinary citizens in the early centuries of the church. We are told by Gregory of Nyssa in a celebrated passage in his sermon *On the Divinity of the Son and of the Holy Spirit*, that 'if you ask about change, they speak philosophically to you about the Begotten and the Unbegotten. If you ask about the price of bread, the reply is, "The Father is greater, and the Son is subject to him"'[32]. The question which lay at the heart of their enquiry was the extent to which the nature of God could be defined. Was the divine nature capable of definition as 'the ingenerate One'? But if God could be so defined, it was clearly impossible for the Son to be divine. What is not clear is whether their primary interest lay in the assertion of

---

[32] Gregory of Nyssa, *On the Divinity of the Son and of the Holy Spirit*, GNO, X., 2: 120,4 ff.

the majesty and aloneness of the supreme God, or in the desire to subordinate the Son to him.

But apart from the desire to clarify theology by means of some definitions, did anything more lie at the root of the Anomoean approach? Were they Aristotelian philosophers in the clothing of Christian theologians? This was certainly the position taken with which to discredit them by their central critics and fellow country men, the Cappadocian Fathers, for whom they were little more than expert logic choppers or technologues. How fair is this critique? Wiles persuasively suggests that, far from being heretical philosophers, the Anomoeans were defenders of the divine accessibility, basing themselves on God's own self definition at Exod. 3.14 'I am who I am'.[33] And by contrast, were the Cappadocians themselves free of all philosophical content and interest and so able to criticize the enemy without embarrassment?

The conventional picture of Eunomius and of his master Aetius as logic choppers derives largely from the writings of his major critics, above all the Cappadocian Fathers. According to them the Anomoeans or Neo-Arians were expert technicians, above all masters of logic devoid of a truly religious approach and not theologians at all. The reason for this is stated to be that they were too much under the influence of Aristotle, never a favourite with the Fathers at least from the time of Tatian, because of his supposed denial of sublunary providence and of the immortality of the soul. At times he is even labelled an atheist. In his first *Theological Oration*, Gregory of Nazianzus writes of Aristotle's 'small minded providence'[34]. On several occasions in his lengthy treatises *Against Eunomius*,[35] Gregory of Nyssa attributes the theology of Eunomius and of the Anomoeans in general to an unchristian acceptance of the philosophy of Aristotle. It is quite striking that this same Gregory, in his own exposition of Christian doctrine for the benefit of catechists, written perhaps in 385, the *Catechetical Oration*, is eager to defend the doctrine of the Incarnation from the charge of

---

[33] M. F. Wiles, 'Eunomius: hair splitting dialectician and defender of the accessibility of salvation' in *Essays in honour of Henry Chadwick*, ed. Rowan Williams, (Cambridge, 1982).
[34] Gregory of Nazianzus, *Theological Oration 1*, Section 10.
[35] Gregory of Nyssa, *Against Eunomius*, 1: 46 and 2: 411.

effectively attributing to Christ an unworthy idea of God by making the divine unjust or not good or lacking in wisdom or power.

However, when we come to look at the actual Creed of Eunomius and compare it with the at times highly philosophical language of all the Cappadocians, it is hard to believe that the slur on Eunomius, though justified as to the body of his actual views, is quite fair to his actual theology. The Eunomian *Confession of Faith* appended to the manuscripts of his *Apology* does indeed insist on the simplicity and unbegun character of the One Supreme God. Eunomius echoes Arius in the ambiguous position he assigns to the Son and in his use of Prov. 8.22 with which to support his case. But there is little if any peculiarly philosophical jargon in his Creed. He insists like Arius on a relationship of will 'by will alone', rather than being, in defining the relation of the Father to the Son. In other words, aside from the desire to structure his belief in a coherent form, there is nothing particularly philosophical in the theology of Eunomius or of his master, Aetius. A sentence from this *Confession* reveals much. 'God did not make use of his own essence in begetting, but rather what he willed, such he begot'. It is indeed true that in Section 20 of his *Apology*, Eunomius writes of a sharp distinction between the respective essences of Father and Son, but in his elaboration of their differences, he on the whole confines himself to scriptural language. He is even prepared to echo Jn 1.18 in 'Only-begotten God', but apart from his rejection of identity or similarity of essence, that is both of the strict Nicene and of the Homoeusian position in Section 22, it would be hard to find in Eunomius the use of strongly marked philosophical ideas.

There is one remaining area of the Anomoean position, which does indeed seem to derive from philosophy – the theory of language. This goes back to an ancient discussion about the nature of the relationship between words, ideas and things. This had already been treated by Origen at *Contra Celsum* 1: 24, where he writes about 'the nature of names'. The problem is whether, as Aristotle thinks, names were given by arbitrary determination, or as the Stoics think, by nature, the first utterances being imitations of the things described. Interestingly, Origen makes no reference to the *Cratylus* of Plato.

The relevance of this discussion to talk about God is clear. Are expressions like 'unbegotten' revealers of the inner nature of God or merely helpful semantic markers indicating without defining? Eunomius clearly held the former view. He writes:

When we say "Unbegotten", then, we do not imagine that we ought so to honour God only in name, in conformity with human invention; rather in conformity with reality, we ought to repay him the debt, which above all others is most due God: the acknowledgement that he is what he is.[36]

Is this attitude to language Eunomius own invention? In his reply, *Against Eunomius*, Gregory of Nyssa suggests that Eunomius owes this insight to a dialogue of Plato entitled the *Cratylus*, which deals precisely with this issue.[37] In the *Cratylus*, Socrates speaks as follows: 'The giving of names can hardly be a trivial matter, or a task for trifling or casual persons and Cratylus is right in saying that names belong to things by nature'.[38] This is clearly not a position that Gregory himself is prepared to adopt, and his attribution of the Eunomian theory to a Platonic source is another instance of his attempt to discredit him by suggesting that his views are philosophic rather than Christian in origin.

It may well be that Gregory is correct in this attribution, though it is worth noting that the actual citation[39] made by Gregory bears little verbal relationship to the *Cratylus*. It clearly was a commonplace of controversy to attribute the views of the opponent to philosophy. Eunomius himself is credited with ascribing Basil's low view of providence to the influence of Aristotle.[40] We have come across this sort of thing before and do not have to take it at its face value.

It is instructive to compare Eunomius' relatively sober use of philosophical language with a writer from Alexandria, whose works were never censured despite their clear addiction to philosophy. Shortly before the outbreak of the Christological conflicts of the fifth century, there arose in Egypt the intriguing figure of Synesius of Cyrene, who became Bishop of Ptolemais in the early fifth century in about 410. He is sometimes termed 'the Platonist in a mitre'. He had been a pupil of the Neoplatonist philosopher, Hypatia, who was subsequently lynched by a Christian mob in 415, an event of which the disgraceful details are recorded for us by the

---

[36]Eunomius, *Apology*, 8.
[37]Gregory of Nyssa, *Against Eunomius*, 2: 404–405.
[38]Plato, *Cratylus*, 390d.
[39]Gregory of Nyssa, *Against Eunomius*, 2: 403.
[40]Eunomius, *Apologia Apologiae* 2, 345: 25–29. See also Basil, *Contra Eunomium* 1, 5 and 9.

church historian Sozomenus.[41] The appointment of Synesius was distinctly unusual. He refused to abandon either his wife or certain unequivocally Platonic beliefs like the eternity of the world and the pre-existence of souls. So he wrote to his brother in 409: 'If I am called to the episcopate, I declare before God and man I refuse to teach dogmas that I do not believe'.[42] It is instructive to see that it was for ideas such as these that Origen was censured together with others like them, both in the nine canons of 543 and later in the fifteen anathemas in the second council of Constantinople of 553. By contrast, Synesius, despite his evident Platonism, was never officially censured for it.

The Person of Christ

Apollinarius of Laodicea (310–390)

A further example of the common tendency to attribute heretical views to the undue influence of philosophy is provided by the case of Apolinarius, Bishop of Laodicea from about 360 till 375, when he seceded from the church. He has been described by an eminent authority as the most brilliant theologian of the fourth century, which is quite a claim when we consider that the Cappadocian Fathers all belonged to the same period. He shared with his friend and ally Athanasius a thoroughly orthodox belief in the divinity of the second person of the Trinity.

His attitude to the person of the Incarnate Christ was determined by two primary considerations, that the divine Christ was one person and that Christ was also sinless. Neither proposition was felt by Apollinarius to be compatible with the possession by Christ of a human soul. If he did have a human soul or intelligence, how was that possible in a being who was manifestly only one person? And if he was sinless,[43] this was an affirmation of his inability to sin, rather than simply of his not having sinned. Such sinlessness was impossible in a truly human figure. The upshot of all this was

---

[41]Sozomenus, *Ecclesiastical History*, book vii, Chapter 15.
[42]Synesius, *Letter* 105.
[43]A truth affirmed at Jn 8.46 'Which of you convinces me of sin?' and Heb. 4.15, 'He became like us in all things, except sin'.

that Christ was without a human soul. Apolinarius offered his own structure of Christ which showed him to be both one person and also sinless. He achieved this by denying the possession by Christ of a rational soul. For this he was condemned and it was and is often claimed that the source of his error was his use of Neoplatonist philosophy as distinct from his own biblical perceptions.

A late fourth century writer Nemesius, Bishop of Emesa, claims in the opening chapter of work *On Human Nature* that Apolinarius owed his views to Plotinus. According to Nemesius, Plotinus held that every human person was composed of three elements, body, soul and spirit, 'and in this he was followed by Apolinarius, bishop of Laodicea'. It is true that at least in the end, Apolinarius adopted a tripartite division of human nature. But it seems equally possible that he derived his views from Saint Paul who offers a nearly similar tripartite division, writing: 'May your spirit, soul and body be kept sound and blameless at the coming of our Lord Jesus Christ',[44] though where Paul has spirit, Apolinarius has mind. The passage in Plotinus offered by the editor of the *Teubner Nemesius*, Morani, as a parallel is suggestive. Plotinus writes: 'And towards the Intellectual Principle, what is our relation? By this I mean The Intellectual Principle itself (Divine Mind). This also we possess at the summit of our being'.[45] Where Paul had spirit, Plotinus has the divine mind. On the face of it, the Christ of Apolinarius has more of Plotinus in him than Paul.

On this analysis, the Apolinarian Christ is the Plotinian human being. Apolinarius has fused the spirit of Paul with the Mind of Plotinus to achieve his theological purpose – the unity and sinlessness of Christ. If, as seems probable, Apolinarius was indeed influenced in his Christology by Plotinian anthropology, there is even so between the two a significant difference. The Apolinarian Christ is unique; Plotinian man is not so. Indeed it is not improbable that we can find a critique of the particularity of the Incarnation, when Plotinus writes: 'It is not by contracting the divine into a unity but by displaying its exuberance that we show the knowledge of the might of God'.[46]

---

[44] 1 Thess. 5.23.
[45] Plotinus, *Ennead* 1, i: 8–9.
[46] Plotinus, *Ennead* 2, 9: 9–35.

Ephesus and its Antecedents:
Cyril and Nestorius

Many conventional accounts of the dispute between the 'Antiochene' and 'Alexandrian' schools of theology are apt to suggest that the basic disagreement between the two depended both on the attitude they adopted towards the interpretation of scripture, whether it was allegorical (in Alexandria) or literal and historical (in Antioch) and on the seriousness with which the two sides took the humanity of Christ, and the differing accounts of salvation that the two visions imply. However, when we look at the evidence for Nestorius' views, a further emphasis emerges. To Nestorius and to the Antiochenes in general, what above all disturbed them in the insistence of Cyril on the unity of Christ, expressed in the title of Mary as Theotokos, Mother of God, was the thought that such a title implied dependence and suffering of some sort on the part of God. How could it be possible to affirm that the eternal divine Word of God was at one and the same time both above suffering, *apathes*, and yet weak and frail and ignorant. Nestorius' strong opposition throughout his all too brief episcopate (428–431) to all forms of Arianism made him sensitive to the Arianism implied as he supposed, in the unitary model of Christ proposed by Cyril.

Nestorius was not by any means the first to feel this difficulty. In his *Catechetical Oration*, Gregory of Nyssa on several occasions feels himself obliged to show how the eternal son could have become incarnate without becoming the victim of *pathos*.[47] To be in any way, shape or form acted on from outside was unworthy of God. But human birth implied as much, therefore the Incarnation was an impossibility. Gregory's reply is to insist that the divine is indeed above all weakness, but he then goes on to insist that although the divine in Christ may indeed be subject to physical change and weakness, it is not subject to moral frailty. What affects the will and perverts it towards evil and away from virtue is weakness, properly speaking. On the other hand, the successive changes we observe in nature as it proceeds on its journey are more properly referred to as modes of activity than of weakness.

---

[47]Gregory of Nyssa, *Catechetical Oration*, Chapters 15 and 16.

But the question may reasonably be asked, why should we assume the divine *apatheia* in any case, especially in view of the fact that the portrait of God offered by the bible is hardly of a God who has no concern with us or is without passion or pity? Max Pohlenz argued that the 'taming' of those passages in scripture which ascribe anger to God was the direct result of the infiltration of Greek into biblical thinking by means of authors like Clement of Rome,[48] who appears to be the first Christian writer to speak of God, probably under Stoic influence, as being 'without anger'[49] and, more profoundly, Origen. In other words the problem goes back much further than the challenge presented by the incarnation of God.

The argument is clear and persuasive. That the bible ascribes anger to God is clear from 2 Sam. 6.8, where we read that 'The Lord's anger had broken out upon Uzzah'. And in the New Testament, Saint Paul speaks of the 'anger of God'.[50] But such a divine characteristic was clearly offensive to the more refined Greek philosophers. Plato, Aristotle and the Stoics were at one in regarding the lack of self mastery implied by pathos as unworthy of man and even more of God. How then were the more philosophically minded Christians to defend the sacred text against the charge of offering a vision of the divine which fell short even of the human ideals enshrined in Stoicism as we read in the *Handbook* of Epictetus?[51]

Origen devotes a long section of *Against Celsus* to dealing with this particular difficulty.[52] On the one hand, he can scarcely deny the plain sense of scripture. But he claims that the anger predicated of God, 'O Lord rebuke me not in thine anger';[53] 'Correct me Lord, but not in thine anger'[54] and 'The anger of the Lord was enkindled against Israel',[55] do not refer to any passion God may possess. Rather, it refers to the harsher method of dealing with those who are in need of correction. A similar explanation is offered of Rom 1.18 in book 1: 16 of his *Commentary on Romans*, where the anger of God is referred to the punishment of those in need of it.

---

[48]Max Pohlenz, *Vom Zorne Gottes [On the Anger of God]*, 1909.
[49]1 *Clement* 19.
[50]Rom. 1.18.
[51]Epictetus, *Handbook*, Section 29: 7.
[52]Origen, *Against Celsus*, 4: 72.
[53]Ps. 6.1.
[54]Jer. 10.24.
[55]2 Sam. 24.1.

In short, by the middle of the second century AD, the dictum 'the divine is above suffering' had come to be accepted as part of the 'definition of the divine nature' outside and inside the church. It is even now enshrined in the first of the 39 Articles of the Church of England as 'God has neither body parts nor passions'. This philosophical assumption, rather than any great concern for the historical Jesus, lies at the heart of the Nestorian unease with the Cyrilline assumption that it was the divine Logos that was two or three months old, and died on the cross. How could any feebleness or moral infirmity, like anger or suffering be attributed to the divine nature? Nestorius totally rejected the term *Theotokos* as applied to Mary on the grounds that 'it is impossible for God to be born of a human being'. In his reply to and critique of the *Second Letter of Cyril*, he accuses him of inconsistency and has this to say: 'For the one who was first proclaimed impassible and incapable of a second birth, was somehow reintroduced as passible and newly created'.[56]

Cyril's reply to this critique of his position, which is enshrined in his *Second* and *Third Letters to Nestorius*, interestingly does not challenge the principle from which Nestorius challenges him. He insists that the union between divine and human in Christ is a hypostatic union as distinct from one of divine favour or good will.[57] He makes it absolutely clear in Section 5 of the same letter that he also believes that God is impassible. Where the two differ is in the attribution by Cyril of real suffering to the whole Christ that is body, soul and divinity, leaving his divinity untouched by suffering. This was insufficient for Nestorius, who divided Christ to give more place to the real spiritual and human sufferings of Christ and so to the reality of his historical character, while at the same time protecting the divine impassibility. To the questions 'Who was born in Bethlehem?' or 'Who died on the cross?' Nestorius' reply is either simply Christ or his human nature, while Cyril's reply is God. The classical assumptions behind each writer are the same. Both assume the divine impassibility. It is in their exploration of how this presupposition applies to the person of Christ that they differ.

What is further worthy of note is that as Henry Chadwick suggests, in his effort to make philosophical sense of the Incarnation Cyril

---

[56]*Nestorius* – Reply to Cyril, *letter 2*, no. 220. *Creeds, Councils, Controversies.*
[57]Cyril, *Letter 2*, Section 3.

employed categories whose home is Plotinus and Apolinarius.[58] The Plotinian picture of human nature is of a being that has, as it were, his head in heaven and his feet on earth. On the one hand he is an intellectual perfect spirit, and on the other he has emotions and feelings and a body. How can both be fitted together into a single person?

This problem is addressed in *Enneads* 3: 6 entitled 'The impassivity of the unembodied'. For Plotinus the immateriality of the soul excludes any influence upon it of bodily or emotional states. His conclusion is stated clearly, 'that the Intellectual Essence, wholly of the order of Ideal Form, must be taken as impassive has been already established'.[59] Plotinus' consistency on this matter is well illustrated by his statement that even the human soul is not entirely immersed in the body. 'Even our human soul has not sunk entire. Something of it is continually in the intellectual realm'.[60] In other words there is always part of every human being that rises above the emotions of the lower soul and the body. The presence of the impassible spirit in the body/soul complex is not proof of its having lost its impassibility.

Cyril's knowledge of Hellenistic literature was considerable and, as Chadwick implies, he may have read Plotinus. He was certainly minutely acquainted with the writings of Julian as his lengthy refutation of him in his *Against Julian* shows. After all, there was a flourishing Neoplatonic academy in Alexandria under the leadership of Hypatia at this period. His language both in his *Letter to Nestorius* and in his *Scholium 8* rather suggest some acquaintance with the *Enneads* as he offers a similar solution to the same problem as faced Plotinus. The presence of the impassible Word in a human being composed of body and soul to form one person need not threaten the divine immutability and freedom from passion and sin. 'The impassible was in a suffering body'.[61] If the above argument works, it will reinforce the general position of this book that the 'orthodox' far from avoiding philosophy were more apt to use it than their theological enemies. Both Nestorius and

---

[58]H. Chadwick, 'Eucharist and Christology in the Nestorian controversy', JTS, 1951.
[59]Plotinus, *Enneads*, 3: 6.
[60]Plotinus, *Enneads*, 4: 8.
[61]Cyril, *Second Letter to Nestorius*.

Cyril insist that the divine side of Christ was impassible. Cyril goes further in offering an account of how this can be so in the context of the Incarnation.

The Council of Chalcedon

The fourth great ecumenical council of the church met on the European side of the Bosphorus on 8 October 451 at the behest of the new emperor, Marcion and his consort Pulcheria, the former emperor Theodosius the Second's imperious sister. The political aim of the council was clear, to retrieve the damage done to church and state by the doctrinal disagreements that had pervaded the church since the Council of Ephesus, and so to produce a formula upon which the vast majority of the assembled bishops could agree.

The interest of both emperor and bishops is well illustrated by their canonizing both the *Second Letter* of Cyril *to Nestorius* and the so called *Formula of Reunion* of 433, and of the *Tome of Leo* together with the creeds of Nicaea and Constantinople. Though these four sets of documents in no way contradict each other, the Cyrilline letters stress the unity of Christ, while the *Tome* insists more on the distinctive character of the two natures and interestingly owes a distinct debt to the language and ideas of Tertullian. 'We observe a double quality, not confused, but combined, Jesus in one person God and man'.[62]

The question naturally arises if it is possible to extract from the council a coherent formula, or does it leave the two positions side by side without attempting to adjudicate between them? Did the council in its concluding formula apply philosophical ideas to the issue? In order to clarify the issue, the council made use in its concluding statements of the famous four adverbs 'without confusion, without change, without division and without separation'. According to Chadwick the four adverbs were inserted at the instance of Basil of Seleucia.[63] But we can go a little further.

The question arises did Basil's 'invention' of these four adverbs imply dependence on philosophy of some sort, above all on the philosophy of the later Platonic philosopher, Proclus (412–485),

---

[62]Tertullian, *Against Praxeas*, Chapter 27.
[63]H. Chadwick, *The Church in Ancient Society*, p. 580.

who was roughly contemporary with the council? In his *Elements of Theology*, probably an early work, and therefore before 451, Proclus discusses the unity and composite nature of the soul, where he uses language reminiscent of the definition of 451 with which to make his point. He writes as follows: 'but if all are together in one being devoid of parts, they interpenetrate one another; and if they exist severally, they are on the other hand *distinct* and *unconfused*'.[64] Again, as Chadwick remarks: 'In Proclus' *Commentary on the Parmenides* (129a) the same negative adverbs occur, which enter the Chalcedonian definition'.[65]

These examples may not count as strict proof of dependence. They are, however, enough to reinforce the suggestion that the Fathers of Chalcedon were not in total ignorance of the philosophical world around them, or if not of the contemporary philosophical scene, at least of the background out of which the ideas of Proclus also sprang. The hostility of Proclus to the new religion of Christianity, which is reflected in *Life of Proclus* (412–485) by Marinus, was no bar to the use of his writings by Christians. It was one-way traffic.

Denis the Areopagite and Proclus

This last point is well illustrated by the case of Denis the Areopagite. He was supposed for a long time to be the same man as was converted by Saint Paul on the Areopagus,[66] and it was owing to this erroneous assumption that his writings owed their considerable authority. But in fact 'the anonymous eccentric', as Dodds terms him, did not come from the first century AD at all. The first clear mention of him occurs in the Acts of a council held at Ephesus in 532. Chadwick has this to say: 'Dionysius' primary motive in writing was to domesticate within the Church the mystical Neoplatonic terminology of Proclus'.[67] He never once mentions his name.

Like Synesius of Cyrene before him, he seems to have taken this ideal at times to extremes, above all in his insistence at the beginning of the opening chapter of *The Divine Names* on the

---

[64]Proclus, *Elements of Theology*, proposition 197, (my italics).
[65]H. Chadwick, *The Church in Ancient Society*, p. 582.
[66]Acts 19,34.
[67]H. Chadwick, *East and West, The Making of a Rift in the Church*, p. 60.

absolute simplicity of God. 'Indeed the inscrutable One is out of the reach of every rational process. Nor can any words come up to the inexpressible Good, this One, this source of all unity, this supra-existent Being'.[68] Elsewhere Denis can be read as suggesting that the One is prior to the Trinity: we read that the simple One is manifested as three persons.[69]

Late nineteenth century scholarship established his dependence upon Proclus and the index of the *Corpus Dionysiacum*[70] leaves little doubt about the importance of Proclus for appreciating Denis: ten columns of passages from Proclus are cited.

That Proclus exercised considerable influence on a Christian writer is now generally admitted, nor did it stop there. The anonymous late fourteenth century author of *The Cloud of Unknowing* also wrote a small work with the title Denis hid Divinity, which is a translation of Denis' *Mystical Theology*. The very fact therefore that a Christian writer, however mysterious his provenance and date, was happy to use the works of a pagan author with a decided hostility to Christianity – in common with many pagans Proclus never mentions Christians by name – with which to explore his faith is enough to remind us that Christians were less hostile to pagans than were pagans to Christians, a pattern with which one is familiar from the second century onwards at the latest. In fact, as Chadwick suggests, it was the attempt on the part of Christians to make the philosophy of the Greeks their own that provoked the outburst of Celsus in his *True Account*.[71] Pagan resentment clearly did not die with the triumph of the gospel. It may even have been increased by it.

Plotinus himself, despite his evident hostility to Christianity,[72] almost certainly provided a framework with which Christians could articulate their faith. In his discussion of the intellectual principle, he suggests that the 'intellectual beings are all one and yet distinct, none of them merged into each other'.[73] This sort of language provided a structure which was useful both for defining the unity

---

[68]Denis the Areopagite, *The Divine Names*, Chapter 1, Section 1.
[69]In Section 4 of the same Chapter 1.
[70]'Index' in *Corpus Dionysiacum*, vol. 2, Heil and Ritter (eds).
[71]See Chadwick in his introduction to the translation of *Contra Celsum*, note 409, page xx.
[72]Especially Plotinus, *Enneads*, 2: 9.
[73]Plotinus, *Enneads* 5, 9: 6.

of the Trinity and for the unity of Christ, and may well lie behind both Proclus and Chalcedon.

The same sort of influence is even more evident in Denis's treatment of evil in his work *On the Divine Names* 4: 18–20. Both Denis and Proclus ascribe a similarly negative but necessary character to evil. 'Evil', writes Denis 'is not a being; for if it were, it would not be totally evil. Nor is it nonbeing'.[74] Similar language occurs in the treatise of Proclus, *On the substance of evil*.[75] The treatment of evil is not the only area in which Denis is a beneficiary of Proclus. Like Augustine before him he is happy to use Neoplatonist arguments with which to defend the power and goodness of God.

He appears to follow him also in his insistence on the primacy of the unity of God over the three persons, in other words the Unity of God somehow is prior to the divine Trinity. Such is the implication of the mysterious language of *On the Divine Names* 1:4, which echoes Proclus in *Elements* 4. The supreme deity is described as a monad or a henad, because of its supernatural simplicity and indivisible unity. It is also described as a Trinity, for with a transcendent fecundity it is manifested as 'three persons'. In other words, unity as in all Neoplatonist writers is logically and perhaps even temporarily prior even to the plurality of the Trinity. The transcendent unity of God is also insisted upon in Chapter 13: 3 of the same treatise. The title of proposition 5 of Proclus' *Elements* reads: 'Every manifold is posterior to the One'. Denis is possibly the most extreme example of the influence of later Platonism upon Christianity.

In the area of Christology, we also find Denis owing much to the language of Proclus. At *On Divine Names* 2: 10, he speaks of the transcendent God coming down to our level, while remaining what He is. 'He has come to join us in what we are, without himself undergoing change or confusion'[76] – language reminiscent both of Chalcedon and of proposition 197 of the *Elements* of Proclus. In other words, works and writers as diverse as Denis, Proclus and Chalcedon can be found using very similar language for rather diverse purposes.

---

[74] In Section 19 of book 4: 19.
[75] Proclus, *On the substance of evil* 20:12, 202: 12, 206: 21.
[76] Denis, *On Divine Names* 2: 10.

Concluding reflections

As has already been noted, Christian writers were far more willing to use language and arguments from non-Christian authors and make their own certain Platonic ideas than were the pagans to make a similar use of Christian writings. It must however be admitted that though they were happy to use Greek sources, they did so without making any acknowledgement of their willingness to absorb and refashion ideas taken from non-Christian sources. They were using a licence accorded them by Saint Paul, though the licence was used with varying degrees of seriousness. It also seems to be the case from the late fourth century onwards that this reticence on the part of Christians to admit their dependence may well have been affected by the School Law of June 362 enacted by the emperor Julian, which effectively excluded Christians from higher education.

What has also emerged is that those who came to be thought of as heretics were by no means the only ones to have borrowed from Hellenism. Indeed rather the contrary was the case. 'Orthodox' creeds and orthodox Christian writers, like the Cappadocian Fathers, above all Gregory of Nazianzus (The Theologian) seem to have been more influenced by Plato than were either Aetius or Eunomius by the common enemy, Aristotle.

If the above argument is accepted, it follows that strict adhesion to the literal sense of scripture was by no means a hallmark of those who came to be thought of as orthodox. Far more hostile to the cause of orthodoxy than philosophy was a refusal on the part of Christian authors to use the language and thought of Greek philosophy with which to explore and define Christian belief.

Again the actual mood of the 'heretics' shifts. If it is fair to say, as has been argued, that the reason for the basic flaw in the Arian position is connected with an over literal, arguably Lucianic attention to the actual language of scripture about God, the same is not true of Nestorius. It was his inability to see how Christ could be both divine and human and one, that made him refuse to admit that 'He who lay in the manger was at the same time God from God'.[77] It has been argued that even though Nestorius may have shared some of the interpretative principles of exegesis taught by

---

[77] Cyril of Alexandria, Letter 3 to Nestorius, Section 3.

Theodore of Mopsuestia and his school, this was not the root cause for his condemnation. In his case, it was rather his insistence on the divine changelessness and superiority to passion that forced him to divide Christ. In differing ways both sides to the various disputes were willing and able to exploit the spoils of the Egyptians in order to establish and defend their position.

Finally, if we ask why intelligent and learned men were happy to keep alive the myth of hostility between faith and philosophy, the reason is clear. Certain passages from Saint Paul lay behind such a position.[78] After him, writers like Tertullian, Tatian, Irenaeus, Hippolytus and Epiphanius had given ordinary Christians an anti-philosophical bias, which could only be exorcized with difficulty and which still remains with us. Even so cultivated a man as Ambrose at the end of the fourth century could write to the emperor Gratian in 380 in words that Cardinal Newman cites on at least two occasions: 'It did not suit God to save the world by means of dialectic'.[79] Earlier in the same treatise he had written: 'The philosophers are not believed: the fishermen are. The dialectitians are not believed; the publicans are'.[80] This came from a man whom we know to have on occasion drawn upon the works of Plotinus.

The simpler or less sophisticated Christians who had neither time nor interest in philosophical speculation needed to be respected at all costs. Clever and unscrupulous men like Cyril of Alexandria knew only too well how important it was to have such people on their side. Yet as we have seen, he was as prepared as any to defend his insistence on the unity of Christ by appealing both to the analogy of body and soul and to a Plotinian understanding of the composition of a human person, with head in the clouds and feet upon the ground.

Indeed it is doubtfully possible even for the most entrenched opponent of orthodoxy to create a system which bypasses *all* philosophy. '*Ad fontes*' or 'Back to the bible' had been the rallying cry in Martin Luther's attempt to purify the Christian Gospel from the seductive poison of Aristotle, but even he was influenced by

---

[78] 1 Corinthians 1, 1 Corinthians 2, and 1 Cor. 8.1.

[79] Newman cites Ambrose's *De fide ad Gratianum* 1, 5: 42 at the opening of his 'An Essay in favour of a Grammar of Assent', (1870).

[80] Newman also cites the same passage in Chapter 4 of his *Apologia pro vita sua* and insists by it on rejecting 'paper logic'.

Augustine, the subject of the next chapter. A not dissimilar motive underlay Karl Barth's (1886–1968) more recent effort to purify Christianity from philosophy. His outlook with its rejection of the 'analogy of being' ruled out all use of natural theology. But at least arguably in his case existentialism replaced the classical philosophers of Greece. Theology is impossible without some form of philosophy, and a philosophy which asserts the existence of a supreme being or reality is better adapted to realize this ideal than is a thoroughly this-worldly system.

5

Saint Augustine

Saint Augustine's life (354–430) as it is recounted in his *Confessions* was marked by a double conversion. The first was an intellectual conversion; the second moral. The first was one from the Manichaeism of his young adult life. This philosophy, which had its roots in Persia in the third century AD – its founder, Mani, had died in 276 AD – was dualist and had persuaded the young Augustine, who had already conceived a desire for philosophy as a result of reading the *Hortensius* of Cicero, that matter and the physical universe were not part of God's plan, but were produced by the prince of darkness, who was the author of all evil, spiritual as well as physical.

Augustine had been a 'hearer' of the sect for about nine years from 373 to 382.[1] Then, partly with the help of Aristotle, whose *Categories* he had read at Carthage,[2] he began to be emancipated from their control prior to his conversion to the contemporary Platonism he came across in fourth century Rome. Their influence upon him and his indebtedness to them he freely admits in several places and throughout the course of his long life. In *The City of God*, written well after 413, he writes of the Platonists with great respect, he writes as follows: 'It is evident that none come closer to us than do the Platonists'.[3] This was above all true of their teaching about the spiritual character of the Supreme Being and the immateriality of the soul. In Chapter 12, he is more specific when he writes: 'Among these were the renowned Plotinus, Iamblichus and Porphyry, who were Greeks, and the African Apuleius, who was learned both in the Greek and Latin tongues'.[4] Strangely, perhaps, despite this generous

---

[1] Augustine, *Confessions*, iv, i: 1.
[2] Augustine, *Confessions*, iv, 16–28.
[3] Augustine, *The City of God*, Chapter 5.
[4] Augustine, *The City of God*, Chapter 12.

admission on his part, no subsequent mention is made of either Iamblichus or of Apuleius. So strong was the influence of Plotinus upon him that his biographer, Possidius, tells us that as the Vandals besieged the walls of Carthage, while Augustine was breathing his last, he repeated the words of Plotinus:[5] 'One that sets great store by wood or stones, or, Zeus, by mortality among mortals, cannot yet be very proficient'.[6]

The prior, intellectual conversion was helped to some extent by the systematic doubt he learnt from the Academics, partly, as we have seen, by his reading of Aristotle's *Categories* (translated by Marius Victorinus). Later, in 386, in the retirement at Cassisiacum which followed his conversion, he wrote his three book treatise, *Against the Academics*. In this he argues for the possibility of attaining knowledge against their position of systematic doubt, which rested on the prior assumption that since nothing can be known, therefore assent should in all cases be withheld. Against this position, Augustine argues that some truths can certainly be known, among them logical and mathematical ones. One of the striking features of *Against the Academics* is that it contains only a single reference to Christ towards the end when he writes:

> Furthermore, no one doubts that we are prompted to learn by the twin forces of authority and reason. Therefore I am resolved not to depart from the authority of Christ on any score whatever. I find no more powerful authority . . . I am still confident that I am going to find truth with the Platonists, and that I will not be opposed to Holy Scripture.[7]

Here is a very clear case of the basic assumption of the harmony of reason, as understood by the Platonists and the church and bible.

More significantly in *The City of God* he anticipates Descartes by insisting that 'Si fallor sum' – 'If I am deceived I exist'. He writes:

> I am not at all afraid of the arguments of the Academics, who say, What if you are deceived? For, if I am deceived I am ['Si fallor sum']. For he who does not exist cannot be deceived; and by the

---

[5]Plotinus, *Enneads*, I 4: 7–23.
[6]Possidius, *Life of Augustine*, Chapter 28. Possidius's book was composed less than seven years later.
[7]Augustine, *Against the Academics*, 3, 20: 43.

same token, if I am deceived I am. And since if I am deceived, how am I deceived in believing that I am? For it is certain that I am if I am deceived.[8]

A similar argument can be found in *On the Trinity*, where Augustine writes: 'If he doubts he has a will to be certain; if he doubts he thinks; if he doubts he knows that he does not know'.[9]

The climax and final stage of his intellectual conversion came about through his reading the works of the Neoplatonists, probably of both Plotinus (205–270) and his pupil Porphyry (232–303). As Augustine himself admits in *Confessions*, he had no great love for Greek and his knowledge of these two writers was mediated to him largely through the translations made, again, by Marius Victorinus, a convert to Christianity in about 355 AD.[10]

From these he learnt two important truths.[11] The first was the reality of the spiritual world, with which contact could be gained by intellectual concentration[12] and introspection. Under this Neoplatonic influence took place the only two mystical experiences we know of in his life.[13] Of these, the first occurred before his conversion to Christianity. He was admonished he tells us 'to return into myself'. There 'I beheld the immutable light higher than my mind'. The ideas of the inward journey and of God as the inner light are both ideas that occur in Plotinus' *Enneads*.[14] The similarity between Augustine and Plotinus is illustrated by the following passage which runs as follows:

> What must he do, how lies the path? How come to the vision of the inaccessible beauty, dwelling as if in consecrated precinct? He that has strength and withdraws into himself, forgoing all that is known by the eyes, turning away for ever from the material beauty, that one's made his joy.[15]

---

[8]Augustine, *The City of God*, 11, Chapter 26.
[9]Augustine, *On the Trinity*, 10, Section 14.
[10]Augustine, *Confessions* 1, 14: 23 and *Confessions* 8, 2:3 5:10.
[11]Augustine, *Confessions*, 7.
[12]Augustine, *Confessions*, 7, 16–22.
[13]Augustine, *Confessions*, 7, 10–16 and 9, 10–23.
[14]Plotinus, *Enneads* 1:1; 3 and 8: 6–40.
[15]Plotinus, *Enneads* 1, 6: 8.

Despite Augustine's belief in the importance of the church and sacraments, his early conviction of the importance of the inner life never left him. What he wrote in his early (390) treatise *On True Religion*: 'Do not go outside; return into yourself; truth lives in the inner man'[16] is echoed in *On the Trinity* written more than twenty years later where he criticizes those who look for God outwardly. 'They are trying to go to God by an outer route and forsaking their own inwardness, where God is present more inwardly still'.[17]

The second truth he learnt from Platonism, or rather from Plotinus, was that of the unreality of evil. With this latter weapon in his armour, he was able to dispose of the Manichee argument that evil had a real substantive existence.[18] This movement on the part of Augustine is important as it helped to solve one of the most serious difficulties felt against belief in the power *and* goodness of God. 'If God exists where does evil come from?' Plotinus' influential discussion of this is to be found at *Ennead* 1. 'The good', he writes, 'is that from which all else comes and on which all else depends'.[19] The Absolute for him – he calls it The One – is both supremely real or rather above reality and supremely good. Evil is the result of absence and defect. So, he writes, 'We may at once place evil in the soul, recognizing it as the mere *absence* of good'.[20] This perception of the nature of evil never deserted Augustine, and we find it repeated in the *Enchiridion*, 'For what else is that which is called evil but an absence of good'.[21]

Connected with this is an often repeated view of Augustine that God shows his almighty power above all in his ability to draw good out of evil. It owes much to the view of Plotinus that 'the supreme power can use evil for a noble end'.[22] Augustine on numerous occasions expresses a similar view. He writes: 'Nor would almighty God, since he is supremely good, in any way allow anything evil to exist among his works, were he not so omnipotent and good that he can bring good out of evil'.[23] It is not quite clear how these two

---

[16] Augustine, *On True Religion*, Section 72.
[17] Augustine, *On the Trinity*, book 8, Chapter 11.
[18] Augustine, *Confessions* 7, 5: 7 and 7, 13:19.
[19] Plotinus, *Enneads* 1, 8 Section 2.
[20] Plotinus, *Enneads* 1, 8 Section 11. (My italics.)
[21] Augustine, *Enchiridion* 11 of 420–421.
[22] Plotinus, *Enneads* 3, 2: 5–23.
[23] Augustine, *Enchiridion* 11.

ideas coincide, for if evil is unreal, why does it need to be atoned for or made use of in order to achieve a noble purpose?

Even the mysterious existence of spiritual as distinct from physical evil is something owed to the declension of the Spirit from the Absolute. And here again Augustine's account of this lapse[24] closely echoes that of Plotinus, where he wrestles with the problem of the coming into existence of the Mind/Spirit and souls after the One. 'The evil that has overcome them has its source in self-will'.[25] Where Augustine attributes the fall to pride, Plotinus attributes it to what he calls '*tolma*' or audacity. There is not much to differentiate the two.

In the *Confessions*, Augustine draws up a list of what in his eyes were the significant similarities and differences between the teaching of Plotinus and his school and the fundamental teachings of Christianity.[26] The belief in the existence of a supreme spiritual being and of a divine *Logos* belonged to Platonists and to Christians alike. What the gospel added were above all the self emptying of the eternal Son in the Incarnation, and his cross and resurrection, and the consequent importance of humility both for Christ and for us. Augustine never attempts to conceal his admiration for the nobility and exactness of the Platonists' understanding of the nature of the Supreme Being. They had done so without Christ. So he writes: 'The most eminent heathen philosophers who were able "to behold the invisible things of God, being understood through the things that are made"[27] philosophised none the less without the Mediator, that is Christ'.[28] They had no room or time for either the humility of the incarnation or the shame of the cross. He writes: 'Porphyry refused to recognise that Christ is the principle by whose incarnation we are purified. Indeed he despised him because of the flesh which he assumed . . . a great mystery unintelligible to Porphyry's pride, which the true and benignant Redeemer brought low by his humility'.[29] In a singularly beautiful passage he writes as follows:

> But we, by pressing on, imitate him [that is, Christ] who abides motionless; we follow him who stands still, and by walking in

---

[24]Augustine, at *Confessions* 7, 22.
[25]Plotinus, *Ennead* 5, 1: 1.
[26]Augustine, *Confessions* 7, Chapters ix/13.
[27]Rom. 1.20.
[28]Augustine, *On the Trinity*, 8 Section 24.
[29]Augustine, *The City of God*, 10, in Chapter 24.

him, we move toward him, because for us he became a road or way in time by his humility, while being for us an eternal abode by his divinity'.[30]

Further, as he was later to argue, Christianity insists as had Saint Paul in his speech on the Areopagus in Acts 17.31-32 upon the centrality of the doctrine of resurrection of the body for all.[31] This was specifically against the Platonic notion of flight from the body, epigrammatically expressed as follows: 'True waking up is a true resurrection from the body, not with the body'.[32] This insistence of Plotinus looks like a deliberate critique of Christianity. In other words although Augustine was at one with Platonism in insisting on the importance of the enjoyment of the highest good as the aim of Christian life, he refused to cut off the body from the personality, as Plato had done in the *Phaedo* in order to assure this end. The noble account of the end of the human pilgrimage offered by Plotinus is a flight of the alone (the soul) to the Alone (the One), NOT the resurrection of the body.[33] Bodily resurrection, as Augustine was to insist like Paul before him, lies at the heart of the gospel message. Chapter 5 of book 22 of *The City of God* has as its title: 'Of the resurrection of the flesh, which some refuse to believe though the world at large believes it'.

But despite these important qualifications introduced by Augustine into the cadre of current Platonism, it would be impossible to deny the importance of Platonism for his whole approach, above all for his understanding of the life to come and the movement from faith to understanding. Even if we leave on one side what might be termed the specific teachings of Plato, there exists in his writings throughout his life a Platonic approach. For example, we find Augustine writing:

> For this contemplation is promised us as the end of all activities and the eternal perfection of all joys. "For we are God's sons and it has not yet been manifested what we shall be; we know that when he is manifested we shall be like him for we shall see him

---

[30]Augustine, *On the Trinity*, book 7, Section 5.
[31]Augustine, *The City of God*, 13, 20 and 22, 25 and 26.
[32]Plotinus, *Enneads*, iii; 6: 6–71.
[33]Plotinus, *Enneads* 6, 9: 11.

as he is" (1 *John* 3: 2). We shall contemplate as we live for ever what he told his servant Moses: "I am who I am. And so you shall say to the children of Israel, He Who Is sent me to you" (*Exodus* 3: 14).[34]

Augustine here connects the future hope with the enlightenment provided by God. In the same chapter he writes: 'Contemplation is the reward of faith, a reward for which hearts are cleansed through faith, as it is written "cleansing their hearts through faith" (*Acts* 15: 9)'.

The assumptions underlying the ascent of the mind to God are two. God has planted within each one of us the desire for happiness, which even original sin is incapable of eradicating. 'Even in evils our nature could not lose the appetite for beatitude'.[35] However, the realization of this basic aspiration depends upon both grace and the purification of the eye of the soul[36] 'purifying their hearts by faith' was a favourite text with him.[37]

It is indeed true that the direct vision of God we are designed for is reserved in Augustine for the life to come: it is seen as following upon faith. There are two notable exceptions, both in his *Confessions*[38] before his conversion and that at Ostia with Monica.[39] In much the same way as Plato,[40] Augustine had structured the passage of the serious soul as being from faith to understanding and insight. As Rist points out: 'the most basic principle of Platonic epistemology is not the distinction between 'intelligibles' and 'sensibles' but that between first hand experience which gives knowledge, and second hand experience which gives various sorts of 'belief'.[41] For Augustine there are two distinct though connected senses in which faith is the doorway to the knowledge of God. In this life, we are to employ our minds on the data faith provides and so come to a deeper understanding of what we believe. Secondly the vision of God promised us by Saint Paul is reserved for the life to come.

---

[34]Augustine *On the Trinity*, 1, 7 (*On the Trinity* was begun in 399 and finished perhaps as late as 426).

[35]Augustine, *Enchiridion* 8, 25.

[36]Augustine, *On the Trinity*, 1, 2: 4: 3; 5 (Acts 15.9).

[37]Augustine, *On the Trinity*, 1, 17.

[38]Augustine, *Confessions*, the so-called 'Vision of Milan' in book 7, 16: 22.

[39]Augustine, in book ix; 10; 25.

[40]Plato, *Republic*, Book 6, 511e.

[41]Rist, *Augustine: ancient thought baptized*, (Cambridge University Press, 1994) p. 45.

A similar pattern is discernible, as we have seen, in the scriptural texts for which Augustine clearly has an affection, all of which serve to reinforce this Platonic perspective.[42] A good example of the juxtaposition of many of these texts occurs in *On the Trinity:* 'For we walk by faith not by sight.' Augustine continues:

> Contemplation in fact is the reward of faith, a reward for which hearts are cleansed through faith as it is written (Acts 15.9). Proof that it is that contemplation for which hearts are cleansed comes from the key text, "Blessed are the pure of heart for they shall see God" (Mt. 5.8)'[43].

Even so whatever the source of faith, it is the necessary basis of understanding,[44] and the use of the Septuagint version of Isa. 7.9 'If you do not believe you will not understand'.

Augustine's treatment of a favourite parable, that of the lost son from Lk 15, has several Plotinian echoes,[45] above all in the thought that the journey back to God is not one capable of geographical description.[46] We come close to God or distance ourselves from him by the quality of our desires. On another occasion the same message is proffered in his discussion of the Trinity, when he writes: 'One does not approach God by moving across intervals of space, but by likeness or similarity and one moves away from him by dissimilarity or unlikeness'.[47]

The idea of anamnesis or reminiscence was important to Augustine throughout his life, as a way of explaining the psychological fact that we are often caught between 'knowing' and 'not knowing' – between remembering and forgetting.[48] It is also in evidence in the account of the paradox of research.[49] The fact, he argues in Chapter 1 of that book, that we want to find something out implies that we already possess some inchoate knowledge of it.

---

[42]Mt. 5.8, Acts 15.9, Jn 17.3, I Cor. 13.12, and 2 Cor. 5.6.
[43]Augustine, *On the Trinity* i; viii/17.
[44]Augustine, *De Magistro* 11, 27. Also *On the Trinity*, 15, 2: 2 and Rist pp. 53–58 and 78.
[45]Augustine, *Confessions* 1, 28: 28.
[46]Plotinus, *Enneads*, 1, 6: 8–21.
[47]Augustine, *On the Trinity*, 7, 6: 12.
[48]Augustine, *Confessions*, 10, Chapters 11: 17–18 and 10: 29ff.
[49]Augustine, *On the Trinity*, 10.

However, Augustine offers a critique of Plato's theory of reminiscence as it appears in his *Meno*. He writes, 'The conclusion we should rather draw from the fact of reminiscence is that the nature of the intellectual mind has been so established by its creator that it is subjoined to intelligible things in the order of nature and so it sees these things in a kind of non bodily light'.[50] Even so despite his reservations on the subject, Augustine continued to be influenced, possibly unconsciously, by Plato in his *Tractates on John*[51] of roughly the same period of his development (415–417).

The theory of divine illumination can be treated as a sort of compromise between the 'doctrine' of anamnesis we find in the *Meno* and the natural divinity of the unfallen soul that is always part of the divine world in Plotinus. (And in Plotinus there are no breaks in the spiritual world. All forms a continuum.) The theory of divine illumination is discussed by Rist and Markus:[52] its purpose was to offer some sort of explanation of the fact that all of us experience within ourselves truths and an authority behind the truths which we cannot create ourselves, but which come to us from another. The ideas of justice and goodness are not self-created, and the question of their provenance arises. Today the answer might well be that they are sociologically conditioned. For Augustine, they were a witness to the presence within us of justice, beauty and goodness, greater than our own, for which we are not responsible and which we do not control, namely God.

His enduring Platonism never left him and is above all evident in his frequent insistence that important though faith is, it is not by itself the end point of the soul's approach to God. Rather it is the first stage through which we must pass before we move into the realm of truth or *veritas*. A good example of this movement occurs in On the Trinity,[53] he writes: 'We could not pass from being among things that are originated to eternal things, unless the eternal allied himself to us in our originated condition and so provided us with a bridge to his eternity'. This is our old friend from tractate 13 on Saint John *per Christum hominem ad Christum Deum* (through

---

[50]Augustine, In book xii, xv (24).
[51]Augustine, *Tractates on John*, 69: 1.
[52]Rist and Markus, *History of Late Greek and Early Mediaeval Philosophy*, p. 78.
[53]Augustine, *De Trinitate*, 4, 18: 24, 19: 25.

Christ the man to Christ the God). Christ is the way to the truth and according to *Confessions*,[54] there is no other.

This impression is reinforced by a passage in his *Second Treatise on the First Letter of John*. Augustine writes: 'Hold on to Christ. He became temporal because of you that you might become eternal'.[55] Another passage reinforces this impression. 'But we by pressing on imitate him who abides motionless; we follow him who stands still and by walking in him we move towards him [that is Christ], because for us he became a road or way in time by his humility, while being for us an eternal abode [*mansio*] by his divinity'[56].

This attitude to the relationship of human and divine, temporal and eternal, in the person of Christ is reflected in Augustine's treatment of the sacraments. For him the word sacrament is given the sense of *signum* or sign; a subject discussed by Augustine particularly in the opening sections of book 1 of *On Christian Teaching*. It becomes therefore in his hands one member, albeit a privileged one, of the class of pointers to a reality that lies beyond. In *Sermon 7, 4*, he lists a number of cases of God addressing us through signs, in all of which there is a clear distinction between the actual thing or '*res*' on the one hand and the pointer on the other. His sacramental theology, therefore, is usually, and with some justice, labelled symbolic. In a passage of singular beauty, Augustine writes: 'The hands of men give the sacrament its physical appearance, but it can only be consecrated into being such a great sacrament by the invisible working of the Spirit of God'.[57]

However, this distinction between time and eternity is strangely blurred in places. On this subject it is instructive to compare Augustine's attempt to bridge the gap between time and eternity with the vision offered by Gregory of Nyssa. In *Confessions*, Augustine seems to create an in-between condition for the benefit of the angels, who seem to belong neither to time nor to eternity, but bear a curious similarity to the position occupied by the Word in the system of Arius. There he writes: 'Your host, which is not wandering in alien realms, although not coeternal with you, never the less experiences none of the vicissitudes of time because ceaselessly and unfailingly,

---

[54]Augustine, *Confessions*, 7, 20: 26.
[55]Augustine, *Tractate 2.10 on I John*.
[56]Augustine, *On the Trinity 7*, 2: 5.
[57]Augustine, *On the Trinity*, 3, 10.

it cleaves to you'.[58] It is almost as though he were endorsing the Neoplatonic theorem that 'there are no straight lines across the map of the universe'. So, when Plotinus derives the All from the One, he makes no sharp distinction in this self articulation downwards. 'The highest', he writes, 'began as a unity, but did not remain as it began. All unknown to itself it became manifold'.[59] Despite the strangeness of this account of the production of plurality, the continuity between origin and product never becomes a Christian doctrine of creation.

Gregory of Nyssa distinguishes his own position from this. For him, creatures are all prisoners of time for ever. He denies any intermediate state between creature and creator, and therefore between time and eternity, he writes that one alone, that is God, is outside time.[60]

The difference between these two writers, both operating within the Platonist tradition, is reflected in the different interpretations given by them to the words of Saint Paul: 'Now we see darkly in a glass, but then face to face'.[61] For Gregory, the created spirit, whether human or angelic, never escapes from the realm of faith and time. It is unendingly upwardly mobile.[62] For Augustine on the other hand, the angels are permanently in a condition of some sort of timelessness and, as we have seen, we too, this life over, shall become changeless and exchange the partial knowledge offered by faith for the full knowledge provided after death by the vision of God. This promise of ultimate vision is guaranteed in *On the Trinity*.[63] At the end of his *Enarration on Psalm* 145: 20, he exhorts his readers to 'love eternity'. Finally the stirring passage with which the last book of the *City of God* concludes is a promise and hope of vision. Interestingly therefore, Augustine seems more Platonist than does Gregory, with whom the distinction between created and uncreated, time and eternity, enters more thoroughly into the fabric of his thought. Augustine's understanding of the divine nature and his wrestling with the doctrine of the Trinity shows further evidence of the influence exercised upon him by Platonism, above

[58]Augustine, *Confessions*, 7, 11: 13.
[59]Plotinus, *Enneads*, 3, 8: 8.
[60]Gregory of Nyssa, *Against Eunomius* 1: 217–219 and *Life of Moses* 2: 173.
[61]1 Cor. 13.12.
[62]Gregory of Nyssa, *Life of Moses* 2: 225.
[63]Augustine, *On the Trinity*, 2, 17: 28.

all in its Plotinian form. As we have seen,[64] despite the fact that in three important respects, that is in the Incarnation, Crucifixion and Resurrection of Christ, there is something beyond Platonism, nevertheless the concept of the divine unity owes much to Plotinus. To begin with, Augustine is a great advocate of the divine unity. The first book of his treatise *On the Trinity* begins with the statement that the search is on for 'the unity of the Trinity'.[65] The Son does indeed, as Nicaea had asserted, share the same substance as the Father: but Augustine wishes to go further in insisting on the unity of all three persons. Towards the beginning of his *Enchiridion* he identifies the one God with Father, Son and Holy Spirit.[66] As for Plotinus and for Origen, the idea of unity is central, but while they were in a position to attribute absolute unity to the first principle only and deny it of or to the second principle, whether mind or the Son, this was not an option open to Augustine who believed, in accordance with the creed of 325, that the absolute reality was not absolutely simple. He is also three persons.

His solution to the mystery of how God can be both three and one at the same moment without, as Harnack suggests, lapsing into Modalism, is solved with the help of the doctrine of relationship. Identity implies some sort of difference, which is neither accidental nor substantial. Being either Father, Son or Spirit of both does not tell us about either the nature of the deity or about distinctive accidents – there are none in God – but rather about the way they are relative to each other. 'So we are left with the position that the Son is called being by way of relationship, with reference to the Father . . . just as when you say "master" you point not to a being but to a relationship'.[67]

At the opening of book 8 we read that what distinguishes the three persons of the Trinity is the idea of relationship. What distinguishes one divine hypostasis from another is the relationship they bear one to another. Language very similar to this occurs in Plotinus, who also deals with the nature of relationship. 'Our task is to give full value to the elusive character of relation . . . Relation is not an attribute of another, nor is it a hypostasis by itself. It is

---

[64]Augustine, *Confessions* 7, 10: 13.
[65]Augustine, *On the Trinity*, 3: 5.
[66]Augustine, *Enchiridion*, Section 9.
[67]Augustine, *On the Trinity*, 7, 2.

something quite distinct'.[68] The language of Augustine is very similar. 'Therefore', he concludes, 'although being Father is different from being Son, there is no difference of substance, because they are not called these things substantially, but in relationship to each other; yet this relationship is not an accident, because it is not changeable'.[69]

Augustine and the human will

The influence of Saint Paul and of the Pelegian controversy

Dihle, in his work *The Theory of Will in Classical Antiquity*, suggests that Augustine invented the concept of will as a separate faculty of the mind for the first time.[70] This is perhaps going too far, but it must be admitted that Augustine's whole approach distinguishes him radically from the intellectualism that the Greeks and many of the Eastern Fathers display. The first conversion of Augustine had taken place, as he tells us[71] through reading the books of the Platonists. The second conversion was achieved by means of the letter of *Saint Paul to the Romans* 13: 13-14 in the garden in Milan. He heard, so he tells us, the voice of a child calling out 'Take up and read; take up and read':

> Then I seized the book of the Apostle, opened it and read the first passage. My eyes lit on: "Not in rioting and drunkenness, not in eroticism and indecencies, not in strife and rivalry, but put on the Lord Jesus Christ and make no provision for the flesh in its lusts". I neither wished nor needed to read further.[72]

This experience effectively proved to Augustine that he was not in control of his own will. He could indeed, as he was later to insist, make free choices, but without the help of grace he was deprived of the ability to make good choices. The fact that the earliest account

---

[68]Plotinus, *Enneads*, 6, 1: 7.
[69]Augustine, *On the Trinity*, 5, 5:6.
[70]Dihle, *The Concept of Will*.
[71]Augustine, *Confessions*, 7.
[72]Augustine, *Confessions*, 8, 7: 29.

we have of his conversion,[73] refers to his reading of some of the
writings of Plotinus and contains no reference to Rom. 13.13, or
indeed any reference at all to the writings of Saint Paul, has led
some scholars to argue famously: 'Both morally and intellectually,
it was to Neoplatonism that Augustine was converted, rather than
the gospels'.[74] The paucity of mentions of Christ in *Against the
Academics* led Alfaric to argue plausibly, but unpersuasively, that
the reference to Rom. 13.13 in *Confessions* 8 was inserted into the
account of his conversion by the author at a later date, as a result of
his close reading of the Apostle after his priestly ordination in 391.

A more recent French scholar, Serge Lancel questions the size
of the gap between the *Confessions* and the earlier writings upon
which Alfaric rests his case.[75] Even so, though the argument of
Alfaric is unacceptable, it is still true that the sketch of the Christian
life offered in the earlier part of his *On Christian Teaching*, begun
shortly before the *Confessions* in 395, could not inaccurately be
described as Platonism with a dash of the Incarnation. Later
experience, above all his disagreement with Pelagius from as early
as 412, forced Augustine to modify such a position. External
pressures, above all after his ordination as a bishop in 395 and of
his becoming Bishop of Hippo a year later were a driving force in
the development of his views on both the nature of the church and
of the nature of human freedom and of the grace of God.

Augustine's gradual change of mind above all on the nature
of the human will[76] can be traced in his writings. In his earlier,
anti-Manichee writings, he is eager to defend the freedom of the
will against Manichee determinism. In his *Soliloquies*, written
immediately after his conversion in 386, he uses the language of
Platonism in describing the mind [and ignorance] as the source
of evil choices. '*Deus quem nemo amittit nisi deceptus*' – 'The loss
of God is a result of being deceived'.[77] Education is the key to moral
improvement as it is in the *Protagoras* of Plato. In that dialogue,
Plato argues that 'no one willingly chooses that which he supposes
to be evil'.[78] Education for Plato is the key to the life of virtue.

---

[73]Augustine, *On the Blessed Life* 1, 4, composed in late November 386.
[74]Prosper Alfaric, *L'évolution intellectuelle de Saint Augustin*, Paris, 1918.
[75]S. Lancel, *Saint Augustine* (1999), p. 102.
[76]Dihle, 1982, cf. note 16, p. 6.
[77]Augustine, *Soliloquies*, 1, 3: 3.
[78]Plato, *Protagoras*, 358c.

Knowledge and freedom support each other. Ignorance is vice and virtue is knowledge.

The sovereignty of the will that we encounter at Augustine's early work *On Free Will* (begun in Rome in 387 and completed five years later) is already some distance from the intellectualist calculus of Plato. In it, he writes of the sovereignty of the will in a quite new way, '*quid enim tam in voluntate quam ipsa voluntas sita sit?* (What lies so much in the power of the will as the will itself?)'.[79] For Plato the word for sin and mistake are the same – *hamartia*. Both have the implication of missing the mark and so of getting it wrong. The intellectual element is dominant; Augustine, by contrast stresses the will, whose relation to the mind is never altogether clear. His increasing immersion in the writings of Saint Paul after his priestly ordination in 391 had taught him that sin was more than missing the mark and ignorance. It was rather the responsibility of the will and marked the refusal of submission to the will of God.

In later Augustine, a darker vision of human nature is patent. Partly, though not entirely, under the influence of the controversy with Pelagius, a more sombre, less Platonist understanding of human nature gathers force. The doctrine of original sin, already evident in *Confessions* where it is first explicitly mentioned,[80] becomes a dominant factor in his whole approach. In various places Augustine endeavours to account for original sin in a way distinct from Platonic rationalism. In *The City of God*,[81] Augustine attributes the evil actions of Adam and Eve to the 'evil will which preceded man's evil acts. This evil will was the tree which bore fruit in evil acts'. In Chapter 13, we learn that the origin of the evil will was pride, that is the desire to set oneself up as a rival to God, to which is added the idea of *superbia* as the ultimate source of all evil.[82] And this idea persists through the mature Augustine, as at *Enchiridion*, where the fall of the angels also is attributed to *impia superbia*.[83] Had the angels and Adam and Eve been aware of the catastrophic results of their rebellion, it is doubtful if they would have acted as they did. The will appears to act irrationally. It is a long way from the Platonic

---

[79]Augustine, *On Free Will*, 1, 12: 26.
[80]Augustine, *Confessions*, 5; 9: 16.
[81]Augustine, *The City of God*, 6, 11.
[82]Augustine, *The City of God*, 12, 6.
[83]Augustine, *Enchiridion*, 28.

and Aristotelian visions of life where information leads to moral improvement and where no one willingly makes a mistake, which for Plato means nearly the same as the Judaeo-Christian notion of sin. To the insistent question, 'Why did God *not* prevent sin in the first place', Augustine's insistent reply is always the same: 'God did not deprive man of the power of free will, because he at the same time foresaw what good he himself would draw out of evil'.[84] 'God shows his power above all in his ability to draw good out of evil'.[85]

Even so the notion of total depravity is never registered in Augustine in the sense in which some of his sixteenth century followers, above all Luther and Calvin, did. Despite his increasing insistence on the impotence of the human will and its endemic frailty and his gradual abandoning of the optimism of the *Soliloquia* and *On Free Will* in favour of a less rosy view of human existence, he never rejected the value of the human intelligence, either in this life or in that to come. For Augustine even the wounding of the will caused by the fall seems hardly to affect the mind. In other words, although the sense of human impotence and of the need of divine grace becomes ever more urgent, the image is never entirely effaced. So we find him writing in 412 in *On the Spirit and Letter*: 'Yet we must remember that the image of God in the human soul has not been so completely obliterated by the stain of earthly affections that no faint outlines (*lineamenta extrema*) of the original remain'.[86] A similar insistence may be found in *On the Trinity* of roughly the same date. There he can write: 'And yet in this evil state of weakness and confusion, it could not lose its natural memory, understanding and love of itself'.[87] This means that even after sin and before the grace of salvation, the image of God in man is not totally destroyed. The will may be impotent, but the mind retains its natural sharpness.

The cardinal virtue that is everywhere assumed is the very un-Greek one of humility. This stress on the prime value of humility is well illustrated in a letter written to Dioscorus as early as 411, where he writes that the first, second and third duty of the true Christian is humility even as the primary demand on the orator is

[84]Augustine, *The City of God*, 22, 1.
[85]Augustine, *Enchiridion*, 27.
[86]Augustine, *On the Spirit and Letter*, 28, 48.
[87]Augustine, *On the Trinity* 14, 14: 19.

that of diction.[88] The humility of the Christian should take as its model the humility of Christ. He writes: 'Christ willed to be baptized in water by John, not that any sin should be washed away from him, but to show his great humility'.[89] Later in the same treatise, the humility of God in Christ is to chastise human and angelic pride.[90] Similarly the preface to *The City of God* contains the following sentence: 'I am aware what ability is required to persuade the proud how great is the virtue of humility'.[91] The Greek equivalent of *humilitas*, which is *tapeinosis*, is virtually ignored by Aristotle in his *Nicomachean Ethics*. By contrast, the same work has a good deal to say about *megalopsychia*,[92] that is greatness or magnanimity of soul. The notion of divine humility occurs nowhere.

It is perhaps worth noting that although Aristotle laid little stress on the importance of humility and the dangers of pride, Aeschylus, as we have seen did – when he saw pride as the root cause of the fall of the house of Atreus. 'Ruin is the penalty of reckless crime, when men breathe a spirit of pride above just measure'.[93] For Augustine, pride is less a separate sin than one which lies at the root of all sin. He writes:

> There is pride there, by which the man preferred to be in his own power rather than God's, and sacrilege . . . and murder . . . and spiritual fornication . . . and theft and avarice . . . and all the other sins can be discerned in this one crime by a person who considers carefully.[94]

According to Augustine we appear to lose the power to act in accordance with the divine will (which he calls *libertas*) while retaining the ability to choose (which he calls *liberum arbitrium* or free will) – a distinction for which Augustine seems to have been largely responsible. At times he can be interpreted as denying human freedom in the second sense in this life because he states that as a

---

[88] Augustine, *Letters*, 118.
[89] Augustine, *Enchiridion*, 49.
[90] Augustine, *Enchiridion*, Section 108.
[91] Augustine, *The City of God*.
[92] Aristotle, *Nichomachaen Ethics*, book 4.
[93] Aeschylus, *Agamemnon*, 374.
[94] Augustine, *Enchiridion*, 45.

result of original sin we lose not *libertas*, but *liberum arbitrium*.[95] This, however, may be simply an example of inexact writing.

This frailty of the will is the consequence of the fall and can only be remedied by the gratuitous assistance of God in Christ. In the convalescent home that this world is, we gradually recover the lost grace of paradise until this life ends, when in the next life, freedom acquires an entirely new meaning. There or rather then in heaven, we shall lose the power of turning away from the contemplation of God for which He made us in the first place. This is clear at *Enchiridion* 105, in *The City of God*[96] and in *On Correction and Grace*[97], in all of which it is clearly stated that in the future life we shall not be able to sin, and therefore shall be truly free. Even if Augustine did not invent the notion of the will as a separate faculty, as Dihle argues he did,[98] he certainly treated it more seriously and fully than did his predecessors – both pagan and Christian. The importance of pride and of original sin as its consequence are indeed novel, as is the sharp awareness that understanding will not of itself enable us to avoid sin and achieve virtue.

Conclusion

Therefore we find both continuity and discontinuity between him and his Hellenic heritage in Augustine just as we have found these in his predecessors. In addition we have found in Augustine a tension between the two central factors that define his responses. It is not altogether clear whether he realized this particular tension between Plato and Paul: he confesses both his debt to and difference from the Platonists.[99]

A good example of the unresolved tension existing in Augustine between Hellenism and Paulinism is his treatment of moral evil. On the one hand he believes, in common with Plotinus, that evil is somehow unreal, a defect of goodness. This is a view he retains to the end of his life and is repeated.[100] On the other hand he attributed

---

[95] Augustine, *Enchiridion*, 30 (written in about 421).
[96] Augustine, *The City of God*, 22,30.
[97] Augustine, *On Correction and Grace*, 11, 32.
[98] Dihle, cf. 1989 note 76.
[99] Augustine, *Confessions*, 7.
[100] Augustine, *Enchiridion*, 11–12.

our own choice of evil in preference to good not to ignorance to but to the evil will which preceded the evil act. So he can write: 'For the evil act had never been done, had not an evil will preceded it'.[101] Is it consistent to hold on the one hand that evil is unreal and on the other that it has a cause in the defective human will?

From their self sufficiency and contempt for the body, he distinguishes the Christian respect for the whole of the divine creative activity and the importance of the virtue of humility. Augustine as the doctor of grace increasingly, with the passage of time, came to see the impotence of the human will and its urgent need for the divine help. But he never lost that respect for the mind or that hope that we are made for the vision of God which crowns faith and lies beyond this life. In support of this picture, he is indeed able to deploy many passages above all from Paul and John; but the Platonic hope is never far away. We are trapped as it were between two distinct drives. Platonism had taught him about the upward dimension and movement of the human spirit in its search for happiness in the vision of beauty.[102] Saint Paul taught him above all in the *Letter to the Romans*, that strong though the upward call may be, it remains of itself impotent if it is not empowered by the freely imparted grace of God: 'Who will rescue me from the body of this death? Thanks be to God through Jesus Christ Our Lord'.[103]

And herein lies the essential paradox of Christianity, disclosed for the first time by Augustine. God has mysteriously planted within us a natural desire for happiness, which can only be realized in the vision of God, while at the same time making the realization of that desire depend in the first instance on the gift of grace. Even our merits are his gifts.[104] Or to use the language of the *Confessions* i, 1: 'God has made us for himself and our heart is indeed restless till it rests in him'.[105] Yet in book 10, he utters his famous prayer which acknowledges his total dependence on God: 'Give what you command and command what you will'.[106]

---

[101] Augustine, *The City of God*, 14, 13.
[102] Plato, *Symposium* and Plotinus, *Ennead* 1: 6.
[103] Rom. 7.24-25.
[104] Augustine, *Enchiridion*, 107.
[105] Augustine, *Confessions*, 1, 1.
[106] Augustine, *Confessions*, 10: 29.

6

Epilogue

So far an attempt has been made to explore the interrelation between faith and philosophy during the first five centuries of the life of the church. Throughout the whole period up to and including the Council of Chalcedon, except perhaps in the minds of men like Tertullian and Tatian – and even there, as we have seen, not quite consistently – there existed no violent disjunction between the claims of faith and philosophy, Jerusalem and Athens.

The expansion of Christianity outside the Holy Land took the form of starting with the central gospel message of the person and teaching of Christ, and then with the help of philosophy endeavouring to make it intelligible and structuring it for the benefit of an increasingly non-Jewish community. But the beginning was always some form of primitive *credo*, of the sort outlined by Saint Paul.[1] The sermon delivered by Saint Paul on the Areopagus[2] does indeed begin from philosophy, but seems to have had only limited success, above all when Paul added to the Stoic vision of the world the specifically Christian idea of the resurrection from the dead.

Justin Martyr's account of his conversion in his *Dialogue with Trypho the Jew* does indeed begin with philosophy, but he seems to have been rather an exception. His love for philosophy, he tells us, led him through Aristotle, Pythagoras and Plato till finally he arrived at Christianity – his basic assumption being that Christianity was 'the true philosophy'.[3] 'In the garb of a philosopher', writes Eusebius, 'he served as an ambassador of the word of God, and contended in his writings for the faith'.[4] Indeed it was this black

---

[1] 1 Corinthians 15, 1–4.
[2] Acts 17, 22–31.
[3] Justin Martyr, *Dialogue with Trypho the Jew*, Chapter 2.
[4] Eusebius, *Ecclesiastical History* 4, 11: 8.

philosopher's robe which interested Trypho at the opening of the *Dialogue*. But what is significant is that, perhaps unconsciously, Justin set the agenda for the Patristic period in his selection of Plato as the philosopher who stood closest to the gospel.

Even a writer as adventurous as Origen began his great work *On First Principles* with a rule of faith. Unlike Justin, Tertullian and Clement, Origen was baptized as a young boy and was not converted to the faith in adult life. The basic motto was 'faith first, understanding later'. Like Augustine in *On the Trinity* and later like Anselm, they took as their basic justification for this procedure the words of the Septuagint version of Isa. 7.9: 'If you do not believe, you will not understand'. The opening words of *On the Trinity* state Augustine's method:

> The reader of these reflections of mine on the Trinity should bear in mind that my pen is on the watch against the sophistries of those who scorn the starting point of faith, and allow themselves to be deceived through an unseasonable and misguided love of reason.[5]

The conversion of Constantine in 312, along with its undoubted advantages from the point of view of the church, allowed the emperor to intervene in ecclesiastical affairs in much the same way as his pagan predecessors had done. Constantine may not have shared the actual convictions of Augustus, Decius and Diocletian, but he did believe like them that a healthy civil society demanded a unified religious one. Where belief and politics were so closely united, it was necessary to find formulae that would satisfy as many as possible. Hence in large measure, the third, fourth, fifth and sixth ecumenical councils assembled respectively at Ephesus in 431, at Chalcedon in 451 and Constantinople in 553 and 680–1 were all convened by the emperors of the day, for the sake of political unity as much as for doctrinal exactness. In other words, the doctrinal disputes of the later Christian empire display a fascinating tension between the search for uniformity and the demands of logical coherence in the formulation of Christian doctrine.

---

[5] Augustine, *On the Trinity*, book 1, 1:1.

Platonism

The dominant philosophy throughout this period was Platonism in one of its several incarnations: Middle for Justin and Origen; Neoplatonism for Augustine and a mixture for the Cappadocians. It offered a speculative system especially in its arguments for the existence of a spiritual world, the world of forms and for the immortality of the soul in the *Phaedo, Phaedrus* and the *Republic*. The natural immortality of the soul is assumed by most of the Fathers, though the nature of its insertion in the body was long unresolved. This is clear from *Letter 166* of Augustine, who remained on this topic permanently undecided as between pre-existence and traducianism, that is the handing down of the soul in the moment of conception.

But perhaps more importantly, Platonism offered a spiritual vision that exercised a great influence on all the great Fathers, notably Origen, the Cappadocians and Augustine. Plato's spiritual vision above all with its stress on the ascent of the mind to God as outlined in both the *Republic* and the *Symposium* could easily be harnessed to the ideal of 'Blessed are the pure in heart, for they shall see God'.[6] Platonic influence is above all discernible in the frequency with which the upward movement of the soul as described in Diotima's speech in Plato's *Symposium* is cited. There, the individual strives and is drawn upwards by the desire for absolute beauty. We find this image being employed by Origen in the Prologue of his *Commentary on the Song of Songs*, by Basil in the prologue to his *Rules* and by Gregory of Nyssa in Chapters 10 and 11 of his treatise *On Virginity*.

It is, however, important to remember two features of the attitudes of Christians to extra–Christian culture, above all its philosophy. Ambiguity is the best way of describing their general position. It is particularly noticeable in Tertullian, whose somewhat ambiguous attitude to classical culture has already been noted in Chapter 2.

A similar ambiguity is just as real, though less rhetorically emphasized in Basil. Like Tertullian, though less paradoxically, Basil can, on occasion, refer slightingly to his immersion in classical literature, despite his evident familiarity with the culture of Greece,

---

[6]Mt. 5.8

as a waste of time. He had imbibed much both at the school of Libanius in the capital, Constantinople, and for five years at Athens with his friend and biographer, Gregory of Nazianzus. There even exists a collection of probably authentic correspondence between Basil and Libanius. He even composed a treatise [*Sermon 22*] for the benefit of his two nephews on the restricted value of classical poetry. In this work the criterion offered in deciding whether or not a work of classical literature was to be used by students was strictly moral. Is Homer useful for instructing the youth? This was composed partly to offset the unfortunate effects of the *School Law* passed by the Emperor Julian in June 362, which had in effect required the resignation of all Christian professors of the classics, on the interesting grounds that such a person must of necessity be a hypocrite, professing what he did not practice. Even so, despite this somewhat guarded approval, he can on several occasions refer to his own and Christian interest in classical letters as wasted effort. In his treatise *On the Holy Spirit*, he mentions 'the vain philosophy of the Greeks'.[7] Yet in Chapter 9 of the same work he illustrates his position by language and ideas drawn straight from the *Theaetetus* of Plato. Not unlike Saint Paul, he realized the value, while admitting the limits of Hellenism.

Culture, in the sense of polite letters, was not the only or indeed the primary area in which Hellenism left its mark on Christian writers. We need also to remember that Basil was the first to introduce into the discussion on the Trinity, a distinction between *ousia* and *hypostasis*, which he owed to Chapter 7 of the *Categories* of Aristotle.[8] It is one of the rare instances where Aristotle is employed by the earlier fathers, though granted the low esteem in which they held him for other reasons, the borrowing went unacknowledged.

Aristotle

The influence of Plato is always to the fore in the early Christian centuries, though not always acknowledged. Aristotle by contrast was very different. The index to Chadwick's *The Church in Ancient*

---

[7]Basil, *On the Holy Spirit*, Chapter 3.
[8]Basil, *Letter 236*.

Society contains nine references to Plato; Aristotle is not mentioned once. This is not perhaps surprising. As we have seen Aristotle's philosophy, except in its logical branch, had found little favour with the majority of the Fathers. It is true that Origen's use of the principle of corelatives and Nicaea's and Basil's use of the idea of substance as both individual and generic owe something to Aristotle, above all to his *Categories*. But this was all a tribute to his logical acumen.

The difference between the approaches of Plato and Aristotle is artistically represented by Raphael's painting, *The School of Athens*. In it Aristotle points downwards to the physical universe, while Plato directs us to heaven. One of the obvious weaknesses of Platonism with its emphasis on the transcendence of God and on an accompanying otherworldliness was the difficulty it found in being unable to deal with the more immanent side of Christianity, notably the doctrine of the Incarnation and of the real presence of Christ in the Eucharist.

But despite this, men with agendas as diverse as Tatian in the second century and Gregory of Nazianzus and Gregory of Nyssa in the fourth found Aristotle distasteful, and used him as a stick with which to beat heretics. This was partly for his restriction of the providence of God to non-earthly matters as Gregory of Nazianzus points out.[9] It was also partly because in his *Ethics*, Aristotle had demanded as a necessary ingredient of 'life according to reason'[10] the presence at least in moderation of the good things of this world, which Plato had taught men to eschew, above all in a celebrated passage in which he sketches the fate of the truly just man who wishes to be so rather than to seem so. His life, Plato tells us, will end on the rack and in crucifixion.[11] This passage seems to prefigure Christ in a way that Aristotle's doctrine of virtue as a mean between extremes,[12] fails to. No wonder, as Father Copleston points out: 'Aristotle seemed to some at first sight to have elaborated a naturalistic system in which no room was left for Christianity'.[13]

---

[9]Gregory of Nazianzus, *First Theological Oration*, Chapter 10.
[10]Aristotle, *Ethics*, 10: 7–8.
[11]Plato, *Republic*, book 2 (361e).
[12]Aristotle, *Ethics*, book 2.
[13]Copleston, *Aquinas*, p. 62.

Unresolved tensions

Infinity versus availability

Even with the invaluable assistance of Plato and later of Aristotle certain problems refused to go away. This is peculiarly clear in the challenge presented by the Arian controversy in the fourth century. It resulted in a definition of the eternal relationship between Father and Son. Did that mean that the divine nature could be defined? Or was God beyond the reach of human language?

If we begin with the treatment of God we find in a philosophical writer of the stature of Gregory of Nyssa, we discover that he is prepared to commit himself to two quite distinct positions, which he seems not to reconcile. On the one hand he wants to say that fidelity to the creeds of 325 makes it possible and indeed necessary to define God as a Trinity of persons, Father, Son and Holy Spirit. His whole controversy with Eunomius and with the Spirit Fighters leads to this type of affirmation. There are three hypostases in God. It is to the defence of this truth that he devoted his most lengthy writing *Against Eunomius*, parts of which Jerome heard read at the council of 381.

Yet the same Gregory is probably better known for his insistence upon the divine infinity and in consequence non-availability of the direct vision of God even in the life to come. How the same being of God can be treated as at the same time both beyond definition and yet capable of definition is not discussed. Yet the curious and interesting fact is that in order to deal with the Eunomian contention that the first person of the Trinity can be defined as 'ingenerate' leads Gregory to postulate the divine infinity, which defies any such definition. Yet the enigma is precisely here. The defence of the doctrine of the Triune God rests upon the doctrine that God's nature is beyond definition because it is infinite. How is it possible to believe that God is both beyond the reach of human intelligence and at the same time three distinct hypostases?

This tension is very clear in his treatise *Against Eunomius* where the fact of the impossibility of greater or less infinity is used to argue against the attempt made by Eunomius to grade the infinite members of the deity in decreasing order of power and importance.[14]

---

[14]Gregory of Nyssa, *Against Eunomius*, i, 168, 169 and 236.

It has been argued by Mühlenberg that Gregory of Nyssa 'invented' the idea of the divine infinity. This may not be true. We find very similar affirmations in two sermons of Gregory of Nazianzus of roughly the same date – early 380 or late 379 – and, on the Hellenic side, we find much the same in Plotinus. He writes that: 'The first, [that is the One] is without form and being and is the illimitable nature'.[15]

But it can certainly be stated that he used the idea in his theology more than any other of the Fathers. It is particular evident in his spiritual theology, above all in his *Life of Moses*. There even the angels are committed (in the spirit of Phil. 3.13 'forgetting what lies behind I press on to what lies ahead') to making their way forward in never ending progress.[16] God is infinite, we (and the angels) are finite simply because created. Gregory's understanding of God lies between agnosticism and anthropomorphism, between the hidden God and the God who reveals himself. If one resorts to the device of Basil in *Letter 234* and argue that we must distinguish between the inner nature of God (always beyond our reach because it is infinite) and the divine energies, it must be pointed out that the hypostases belong to the inner nature of God, the energies do not.

In *On the Trinity*, Augustine expresses a similar affirmation of the frailty of the human mind when faced with the divine nature.[17] God can be thought about more truly than he can be thought and he is more true than he can be thought about. What Gregory, Augustine and all the early Fathers lacked in their explorations of the divine mystery was the doctrine of analogy that was adduced by Saint Thomas Aquinas precisely to resolve this difficulty. This is very clearly stated in book 1 question 13 of his *Summa Theologiae* entitled *On the divine names*, above all in article 10. This statement enables one to say in effect, that God is good, but not as we are good, but in a supreme way. Statements about God are neither univocal nor ambiguous but analogous.

---

[15]Plotinus, *Enneads*, 5, 5: 6.
[16]Gregory of Nyssa, *Life of Moses*, 2, 25: 242.
[17]Augustine, *On the Trinity*, 7, 7.

The divinity, humanity and unity of Christ

Unintentionally Athanasius also is vulnerable to the charge of inconsistency or of creative tension in his efforts to deal with the double insistence that Christ is both divine and also one person. On the one hand he is insistent on the importance of the full deity of the Word of God. In fact so strong is his insistence on this that he looks at times as though he denied the human soul and intelligence of Christ having any active or indeed any part at all to play in the work of redemption. 'He became one of us that we might become divine' he writes in his treatise *On the Incarnation*. His belief in the availability of salvation by deification leads directly to his affirmation of the doctrine of consubstantiality of the Son with the Father. Indeed in several places in the same work, it is easy to read him as saying that the divine nature of the Word took upon himself a human body.

On the other hand in his attempt to deal with the critique of his position by the Arians, who alleged certain biblical texts as implying the non-divine character of Christ, as, for example, the reference to his growth 'in wisdom and knowledge' at Lk. 2.52, he adopts a very different strategy. He invokes as a reply the distinction between divine and human in Christ, attributing all weakness to his humanity, none to the divinity. It was only the human nature in Christ that was created and grew and died and rose again.

The Athanasian Christ therefore is a sort of hybrid. The central and characteristic thrust of his reply to Arius is that the Son must be fully divine if he is to save us by making us also divine. If Christ is really to reveal god to us, then all his actions must be divine. Yet when faced with passages which do indeed refer to Christ, and suggest imperfection, we are told that these passages do not refer to Christ's divinity. This leaves us with what was later to be called a divisive Christology. Sometimes Christ acts in his divine character, sometimes in his created reality, but there is no principle at hand to unite the two. It is this sort of incoherence which has led some writers to say of Athanasius that 'he was not much of a philosopher'. Yet both the idea of divinization and the idea of god as perfect and beyond the reach of change owe a good deal to the Greek background which Athanasius must have come across in Alexandria and which influenced him above all in his earlier writings *Against the Pagans* and *On the Incarnation*.[18]

Christian attitudes to their Hellenistic sources

It is perhaps worth remarking that although it is clear that most of the Fathers made use of philosophy, they rarely cite their sources verbatim and hardly ever refer to them, except in a roundabout way. For example, Origen who was arguably the most articulate and best informed of all the Fathers on the philosophical front, having been a pupil of Ammonius Saccas while a student in Alexandria, never mentions his source by name. He only refers to his sources in the one writing which is specifically engaged with Hellenism, his *Against Celsus*. On several occasions in that treatise, he mentions by name the second century Platonist, Numenius of Apamea. His dogmatic treatises never mention Plato though they display a large acquaintance with Plato, as the notes to the German edition make clear. No doubt the differing audiences for which the *Against Celsus* and the *On First Principles* were composed may account for this divergence.

In the fourth century, we find a similar difference between the public Christian face of Gregory of Nazianzus and his private correspondence. So, on at least two occasions in his *Theological Orations*, he offers citations from the *Timaeus* of Plato, the most popular of his dialogues in late antiquity.[19] On neither occasion, however, does Gregory mention Plato by name. He merely says: 'One of the Greek theologians or philosophers'. On the other hand, when we turn to his letters, he makes it clear that he was extremely well versed in Greek literature from the numerous quotations he makes from them in the course of his letters. It may be that the ostensive purpose of his *Orations* precluded too precise a reference to non-Christian writers. Letters allowed more scope for literary vanity.[20]

---

[18]Athanasius, *On the Incarnation*, 54.
[19]Gregory of Nazianzus, *Theological Orations*, 2: 4 and 3: 2.
[20]Gregory of Nazianzus, *Letters*, 30 and 31 to Philagrius, his friend of student days.

But even so generous and cultured a writer as Gregory was reminded uncomfortably of the latent hostility of the Julianic reformation, above all in 362 with the passing of the infamous School Law in June of that year. This law effectively prevented Christians from teaching in schools or universities. Gregory's anxiousness about the possible effects of this attitude is clearly marked in a letter addressed in 362 to his younger brother Caesarius, who was a doctor in the court of Julian. At the close of the letter, he warns him of the choice that lies before him. He must either remain a true Christian and be treated with some contempt at court, or he in his search for honour be prepared to sacrifice what is more important, his Christian faith.[21]

Basil and Gregory of Nyssa were even more reluctant to mention by name the writings they clearly drew upon, except in their private correspondence. Hardly surprisingly neither of them has any sympathy for Aristotle, whom they regard as the source of all heresy, above all that of Eunomius.[22] For them, Eunomius was no theologian but a mere technologue who had learnt his trade from Aristotle. Living as they also did in the shadow of the School Law of Julian of June 362, it is not strange that the name Plotinus never occurs.

But Gregory of Nyssa does surprise by attributing Eunomius' theory of natural language to his study of the *Cratylus* of Plato.[23] On two further occasions in the same work Gregory accuses Eunomius of dressing up his heresy in the elegance of Plato.[24] As we shall see later, this attempt to erase Greek philosophy from among the influences at work on orthodox Christianity did not prevent the Cappadocians from using what they affected to despise.

By contrast, Augustine in the west, is far more precise in his references to and use of the actual names of philosophers as in book 10 of *The City of God*, Chapters 9 to 11 where Porphyry is cited by name.[25] And in the earlier account of his own conversion, composed in November 386, shortly after his conversion and before his own baptism, he attributes it to his having read 'certain

---

[21] Gregory of Nazianzus, *Letters*, 7.
[22] cf. Basil, *Against Eunomius*, 1, 5: 9 and Basil, *Letter* 90 and Gregory of Nyssa, *Against Eunomius* 1, 46 and 2, 620.
[23] Gregory of Nyssa, *Contra Eunomium*, 2, 344.
[24] Gregory of Nyssa, *Contra Eunomium*, 3, 7: 34 and *Refutatio Confessionis Eunomii*, 48.
[25] Augustine, *The City of God*, 10, 9–11.

books of Plotinus'[26] though he does not mention which ones, nor that he probably read them in the Latin translation made by Marius Victorinus probably sometime during the process of his intellectual conversion.

Pagan attitudes to Christianity

On the other hand it is worth noting that this surface reserve on the part of Christian writers, for it goes no deeper, is reflected in a much more definite manner in the attitude of articulate pagans towards the 'new religion'. With the exception of the polemical anti-Christian writings of Celsus, Porphyry and Julian, overt mentions of Christianity are singularly hard to find. These three had to make it their business to know the enemy thoroughly, despite their natural hostility. But even they refrain from calling the enemy Christians, but prefer 'Galileans' or even on occasion 'Atheists'. This is true of both Celsus and Julian, in neither of whom does the word Christian appear, and probably also of Porphyry, the vast majority of whose 15 volume critique of Christianity was destroyed by imperial order in 448.

Even so noble and intelligent a figure as the emperor Marcus Aurelius, who died in 180 never uses the actual word Christian. The apparently highly critical reference to Christians by Marcus Aurelius[27] is probably an interpolation. But the undoubted references to Christians never mention them as such and only obliquely (and unfavourably).[28] What is more surprising is the failure on the part of the historian Cassius Dio, whose history terminates in 229 AD, to make any reference at all to Christianity. This looks more like conscious suppression than ignorance. As Haines states: 'The word [sc. Christian] itself was taboo with pagan stylists as a barbarism'.[29] Real ignorance, therefore, coupled with arrogant contempt, fear and consciousness of possessing a superior culture combined to induce silence on the word if not on the idea of Christianity.

The second century AD pagan writer Aelian (170–235) nowhere uses titles like Galilean or atheist. This is perhaps intelligible granted

---

[26]Augustine, *De beata vita* 1, 4.
[27]Marcus Aurelius, *Meditations*, 11: 3.
[28]Marcus Aurelius, *Meditations*, 1: 6; 3: 16 and 7: 68.
[29]Haines in Marcus Aurelius, *Meditations*, (Loeb), p. 384.

that at that date the gospel had made relatively little headway in highly articulate circles, though it had among the people at large, but it is worth remembering that Justin Martyr was dead by 165, a few years before Aelian's birth. Perhaps also the nature of the subject offered little opportunity for the mention of Christians. Even so we need to remember, as Nigel Wilson points out on page 16 of his introduction to the Loeb translation of Aelian's *Historical Miscellany*: 'The new faith soon produced writers of note, whose works included defences of their beliefs and attempts to win the allegiance of pagans'.[30]

Julian the Apostate habitually refers to Christians as either Galileans or atheists, though he rather grudgingly admits that the Greeks had much to learn from them, above all their organization and charity to which he (correctly) attributed much of their success. His celebrated School Law passed on 17 June 362 had the effect of forcing Christians to surrender their teaching posts in the empire. However obnoxious a move this must have seemed even to pagan writers like Ammianus Marcellinus it raised two important questions. The first was about the compatibility of a pagan education with Christian values. The second was about the integrity and strictly religious character of Hellenism. In this latter point he was clearly following in the footsteps of Celsus, whose *True Account* dismissed intelligent Christians as betrayers of their essentially irrational faith.

In response to his awareness of the need to offer an intelligent account of Hellenism, Julian persuaded his Prefect of the East, Sallutios, in about 362 to compose a resume of pagan beliefs in the shape of a very short treatise entitled *On the gods and the world*. Christians are indeed referred to in the work, but as atheists.[31] The charge used against the Christians in the first two centuries and against which Justin had reacted in his *First Apology*, was still in use two centuries later.

Even more puzzling is the fact that Libanius (314–396), who was a teacher of rhetoric and spent the latter part of his life in the Christian city of Antioch, at no point, either in his *Autobiography* dismissed by Gibbon as 'vain and prolix' or in his letters, refers directly to the Christians. He does indeed make a savage attack on

---

[30] N. Wilson, 'Introduction', *Aelian's Historical Miscellany*, (Loeb), p. 16.
[31] Sallutios, *On the gods and the world*, Chapter 18.

the monks, describing them as 'black robed figures who ate like elephants and drank rivers dry'.[32] Yet he had Christians among his pupils, notably Saint Basil before 350 in Constantinople, and later in Antioch in about 370, Saint John Chrysostom. Indeed there survives in the copious correspondence of Basil, an exchange of letters between the monk and the pagan, some of which are undoubtedly genuine.

And what is true of literary men is true also of philosophers of the stature of Plotinus, who never once directly refers to Christians though attempts have been made to see in certain passages oblique references to Christianity,[33] in *Against the Gnostics* where Plotinus can be interpreted as attacking the Incarnation[34] and the immorality of Christians.[35] His biographer Porphyry, though clearly conversant with Christianity as the fragments of his fifteen volume work *Against the Christians* of about 305 demonstrates, makes no reference to them at all in his *Life of Plotinus*. In Marinus', *Life of Proclus (412–485)*, the fifth century Platonist philosopher refers to Christians only once, obliquely and with hostility as 'enemies of antiquity'.[36] Doubtless it was not easy for the pagans of the late fourth and fifth centuries to be overt in their hostility to what had become the dominant religion of the Roman Empire.

It is a curious feature, therefore, of the early Christian centuries that whereas Christian writers of the stature of Saint Paul, Justin Martyr, Clement of Alexandria and Origen were happy enough to make use of the writings of the classical world, some of them did this without acknowledgement and with some discrimination. Origen in his *Address to Gregory the Wonder worker* and Saint Augustine in *On Christian Teaching*[37] both used as their justification the 'spoils of the Egyptians' of Exod. 11.2 and 12.35.

Their pagan counterparts, with the exceptions of Celsus, Porphyry and Julian, either ignored Christianity or affected to do so, regarding it as an enemy with nothing to offer them except, as turned out to be the case, their own possible extinction. It is

---

[32]Libanius, *Oration* 30.
[33]Plotinus, *Enneads* 2, 9.
[34]Plotinus, *Against the Gnostics*, Section 9.
[35]Plotinus, *Against the Gnostics*, Section 17.
[36]Marinus, *Life of Proclus (412–485)*, Chapter 30.
[37]Augustine, *On Christian Teaching*, book 2.

perhaps worth noting that even Porphyry, the most learned of the three critics, can on occasion use language which, if not derived from the New Testament, is very like it. In his *Letter to Marcella*, his wife, he speaks of the importance of 'faith, truth, love and hope' – a possible echo of the celebrated trio of 'faith, hope and love' of 1 Cor. 13.13.[38] The only difference, apart from the addition of truth, is the word used for love. While Saint Paul uses what may have been an invention of his, namely *agape*, Porphyry like Plato in the *Symposium* speaks of *eros*.

It may be the case that the Greeks deeply resented the attempt on the part of the Galileans or atheists, as they contemptuously termed the Christians, to take over a culture they regarded as their own. In any event the murder in Alexandria in 415 of the pagan philosopher Hypatia and the closure in 529 by the Emperor Justinian of the philosophical school at Athens doubtless fuelled or justified their worst suspicions that Christianity was a religion of anti-culture.

As a footnote to this, it is only fair to point out that the reticence in referring to Christians by name that we find in writers of the Greek-speaking world was not characteristic of the Latin authors. Tacitus,[39] Pliny[40] and Suetonius[41] have no hesitation in referring to Christians by name. The same is true of Ammianus Marcellinus at the end of the fourth century and of Eunapius who, writing of the sophist Prohaeresius says: 'he was reputed to be a Christian'.[42]

How much can be inferred from this discrepancy between East and West is not altogether clear. Perhaps the Eastern pagan writers felt themselves more threatened than their Western counterparts owing to the greater numbers of Christians in the Greek east, and perhaps even to the superior culture they possessed. Certainly the Julianic challenge made thoughtful and cultivated Christians more aware of the problems facing the marriage of Christianity and classical culture than their predecessors had been aware of.

---

[38] Porphyry, *Letter to Marcella*, Section 24.
[39] Tacitus, *Annals*, 15: 44.
[40] Pliny, book 10, letter 96 to Trajan.
[41] Suetonius, *Life of Nero*, Chapter 16.
[42] Eunapius, *Lives of the Philosophers*, p. 493.

Conclusion

In answer to the question, therefore, of the extent to which early Christian writers were influenced by Greek philosophy, it could be stated that the motto 'up to a point' characterizes the whole period under review. Use of philosophy does not of itself mean some form of subservience to it. Saint Paul may have used the Stoic analogy of the body in his attempt to articulate the corporate character of the church[1] but the use of the imagery is not restricted to what he may have found in Seneca.

The same is true of the majority of the Christian writers. In their attempt to define more accurately the nature of Christian belief, the overwhelming majority made extensive use of the philosophy of their own day. Philosophy was an invaluable and necessary ally, but also a dangerous one. It could seek to control rather than to serve. The Fathers and their successors all began from premises derived from the basic gospel of Christ and then tried to show that these doctrines are not at variance with the thinking of the dominant philosophy of the age.

Wise people of all ages and most religions believe in a supreme being or beings of some sort and in the mysterious tension between ease of access and deep mystery that surrounds him/them. To join hands with the inspiring teaching of the Greeks and others is an obvious move. But this can also be a risky business, as Saint Paul perceived when he wrote those stirring words to the people of Corinth: 'Has not God made foolish the wisdom of this world'.[2] And yet it is a necessary move if the gospel is to recommend itself to a thoughtful public, who will not be content merely to accept the preached gospel on the say so of the preached, especially if they do not have other resources of wealth or power at their command.

It is useless, as Origen saw clearly in the third century, to create an unbridgeable wall between faith and reason especially once you are convinced that the revelation made by Christ was made for all men,

---

[1] 1 Cor. 12.12
[2] 1 Cor. 2.6

by one who was at the same time a real historical person, and the Word, and Wisdom and Truth of God. The inspired teachings of the gospel were meant for all people, not simply for a relatively small number of people, whether contemporaries of Christ or those who were drawn from the less well educated classes, incapable either of intelligent questioning or articulate expression of their beliefs.

In this area Origen was by no means innovative. This important truth had been absorbed by Justin Martyr by the middle of the second century. In Section 13 of his *Second Apology* he argues that whatever was rightly said among the followers of Plato 'is the property of us Christians'. It was probably in opposition to so outlandish a claim that Celsus produced his *True Account* in about 175 AD. In the course of this work, preserved for us by Origen in his *Against Celsus*,[3] he claims that Christians are gullible, ill educated people, led astray by scoundrels. For the God the Christian worships is a God who was not only incarnate in Jesus of Nazareth, but also is the Lord of creation and made us reasonable human beings. To claim, therefore, as Luther did, that the image of God has been so effaced in us as a result of the primordial disaster of original sin, may possess certain attractiveness for its simplicity, but closes the door on any rational approach to Christian faith, which is both a difficult and undesirable condition of the human spirit. Despite his low estimate of the moral possibilities of the will of the human creature, Augustine still believed in the value of the human intellect even after the fall. In *On the Trinity* he insists that in fallen human beings the divine image is not lost. 'The human soul is never anything but rational and intellectual'.[4] For Augustine the will may indeed be in need of repair. Not so the mind. And Luther was an Augustinian.

But the attempt to emancipate theology from the clutches of 'alien philosophy', above all from that of Aristotle, can never be wholly successful. Unfortunately any attempt at the domestication of either logical positivism in the Anglo-Saxon world or of existentialism in mainland Europe, are less likely to be tools of a Christian theology. This is largely because the former restricts its discourse to propositions that are either logical or empirically verifiable, while the latter veers in the direction of an immanentist approach, where

---

[3] Origen, *Against Celsus*, i: 9.
[4] Augustine, *On the Trinity*, 14, 6.

the world spirit becomes identified with the human spirit. Even Karl Barth (1886–1968), despite his desire to sever the link between philosophy, culture and the gospel and to create a gulf between the so called analogies of faith and being, found himself influenced by and dependent upon Søren Kierkegaard (1813–1855) with his statement 'truth is subjectivity'.

The fact is that any attempt to emancipate the faith from philosophy then and now is discovered to be flawed. Even the most aggressively anti-philosophical writers like Tertullian turn out on inspection to be much more philosophical in practice than in theory. The real question is therefore, not, 'can we do without philosophy?'. To that question the answer is no. But rather, 'are there some philosophies less and some more apt to act as vehicles for Christian theology?'. The argument of this book has been that Plato and his followers and Aristotle are more appropriate than later ones simply because they point the spirit beyond this world, either to the idea of the good or to self thinking thought. Later ones fail to do this. Discrimination is vital for, as Inge once stated in a slightly different context, 'if the church marries the spirit of the age, she will be a widow in a fortnight'.[5]

---

[5]W. R. Inge, *The Church and the Age*, 1911, Chapter 1.

APPENDIX

In estimating the influence of classical philosophy on the Christian faith it is, perhaps, worth saying that it was only with the gradual rediscovery of Aristotle beginning in the tenth and culminating in the thirteenth centuries that Aristotle's philosophy gained ground. The fact that Islamic scholars from 800 onwards translated Aristotle, with the exception of his *Politics*, into Arabic had in fact an adverse effect on the mind of the West and made him 'theologically suspect'. This suspicion was not really allayed for some time despite Aristotle's adoption in the thirteenth century by Saint Albert the Great, who died at a great age in 1280 and Saint Thomas Aquinas (1225– 1274). Even though the latter never accepted Aristotle uncritically, but only took from him what was in accordance with Christian teaching, suspicion was never far away. And yet, for Aquinas, The Philosopher is always Aristotle.

In three particular areas it is possible to discern the influence of Aristotle on Aquinas: in the proofs of the existence of God; in the discussion of the nature of the soul and of its relationship to the body; and in the understanding of the real presence of Christ in the blessed sacrament.

In question 2, article 3 of his *Summa*, the topic dealt with is the proofs for the existence of God. Saint Thomas advances five proofs: from motion; from efficient causality; from contingency; from grades of being; and from the orderly character of the universe. God therefore emerges as the conclusion of each argument as in turn, the first mover, the efficient cause of all, the necessary being, the supremely excellent being and the order of all. Admittedly the sources of these proofs differ. However, Thomas concludes each 'proof' with expressions like 'this all call God' or 'understand to be God' rather than a more assertive 'therefore God exists'.

The first 'proof' is clearly influenced by Aristotle's proof from motion,[1] where the first mover, as we shall see, moves all else by desire. In Chapter 7, Aristotle describes the intense life of his god, which is 'all thought': 'Therefore life and continuous self existence belong to God, for that is what God is'. This argument of Aristotle assumes that the first mover moves as a final cause, as the object of desire, not as an efficient one. So in Chapter 7 of the same book he writes: 'The object of desire and the object of thought move without themselves being moved'.

It should however be noted that this argument of Aristotle does not end up with creation out of nothing in the sense intended by Aquinas. Indeed it is doubtful if the central question of Aquinas: 'Why does anything exist at all?' would have occurred to Aristotle. To put it slightly differently, both Plato and Aristotle are interested in explaining why things are as they are, not in the more difficult question why do things exist in the first place. Saint Thomas addresses this point in his third proof from contingency. All other things could 'not exist', God and God alone could not not exist. And the existence of God is the condition of the possibility of the existence of all other objects. The proof from grades of being is more Platonic, though Aquinas adduces Aristotle's *Metaphysics* 2 as his source, while the fifth proof from order is more Stoic and had already appeared both in the *Book of Wisdom* and at the end of Chapter 1 of the *Letter to the Romans*.

Aquinas' indebtedness to Aristotle is also discernible in question 76 of Part 1 of the *Summa*. There, in the first article, the question is raised as to whether or not the intellectual principle is related to the body as the form is to matter. Here we find Aquinas siding with The Philosopher against the separatist tendencies of Plato's *Phaedo* and *Phaedrus*, in which the body acts as a prison or tomb for the divine spark. For Aristotle, however, and for Aquinas, the soul is the form of the body, though still at least for Aquinas, immortal – a view with which Aristotle would most certainly not have concurred. This means that despite the debt Aquinas owes to Aristotle, he continues to exploit ideas that appear to imply a rather different pedigree, even as he is much indebted to Augustine before him.

However, in one area at least, Aquinas both parts company from Augustine and uses language and ideas which owe much to Aristotle.

---

[1]Aristotle, *Metaphysics*, book 12.

In his discussion of the Eucharist,[2] Augustine offers a somewhat symbolic understanding of the whole passage. In other words, to the simple question 'what is it that we eat?' the reply comes: 'Why are you preparing your teeth and your stomach? Believe and you have already eaten'. What is important for Augustine is the spirit of faith which we bring to reception rather than what we actually eat.

No doubt in so expressing himself, Augustine displays the general influence of Plato, for whom the real world is the ideal unseen world of forms as distinct from the visible sensible world we see. For Augustine above all, even the sacraments partake of the nature of a sign and like all signs, as he indicates in the opening chapters of book 1 of his *On Christian Teaching*, point beyond themselves. A good example of the Augustinian approach to the Eucharist occurs in *On the Trinity*. He is arguing for the power of God to produce miraculous effects, both sensible and visible in earth, sea and sky. So he writes: '[God can surely act in this way] if he [sc. Saint Paul] could produce meaningful signs to proclaim the Lord Jesus Christ, in one way by using his tongue, in another by writing letters, in another by celebrating the Lord's body and blood'.[3] The idea that God uses different creatures with which to communicate his will to us is not infrequent in Augustine. It occurs in his twelfth sermon. So it is not too surprising to find him using the same principle in discussing the Eucharist.

Aquinas, however, approaches the mystery of the Eucharist from a different perspective, which at once illustrates the influence of Aristotle. The substance–accidents distinction can be found in Aristotle, both in his *Later Analytics* 74 and in his *Metaphysics*,[4] whereas book 12 is 'about substance'. A good discussion of the difference between the two may be found in book 7: 12 of the *Metaphysics*. The definition of a man may be a two footed [or rational] animal, white and black, however, are accidents, which do not enter into the definition of the basic reality or substance. In the *Summa Theologiae* an explanation is offered of the nature of transubstantiation.[5] The argument is that although the outward appearances or accidents of bread and wine remain after the words

---

[2]Augustine, *Tractate*, 25 on Saint John 6: 29.
[3]Augustine, *On the Trinity*, 3,10.
[4]Aristotle, *Metaphysics*, 11, 8.
[5]Aquinas, *Summa Theologiae*, part 3, question 75.

of institution: 'This is my body' and 'This is my blood', the inner nature or substance is altered into the body and blood of Christ. The accidents remain after the change,[6] but the inner reality is altered. How the accidents can continue in a different underlying substance is a mystery. It is therefore, a unique and miraculous change, even as Christ is a unique person. So Davies observes: 'In writing of transubstantiation, Aquinas knowingly uses Aristotle to mean what Aristotle could not have accepted'.[7] In other words, philosophy can be of great help in articulating the mystery of Christ, but only up to a point. Even so, it is important to emphasis that although philosophy cannot give a totally satisfactory account of the mystery it is invaluable as a means of illuminating the mystery of faith.

But Saint Thomas introduced into this thinking a distinction which was to be extremely influential, a distinction which distances him from the whole Patristic era. As Cardinal Ratzinger notes:

The identification of Christianity and philosophy was indebted to a determinate conception of philosophy which gradually came under criticism by Christian thinkers and was finally abandoned once and for all in the thirteenth century . . . a distinction that is largely the work of Saint Thomas Aquinas . . . With a terminology still inchoate in Saint Thomas's works, the domains of inquiry belonging to philosophy and theology were distinguished respectively, as the natural and supernatural orders'.[8]

The consequence of this distinction led to the emancipation not only of philosophy but also of all other branches of scientific knowledge from the control or embrace of theology. It is significant that the shift in interest from Plato to Aristotle seems partly responsible for this revolution. It is worth remarking that Saint Thomas' exact contemporary the Franciscan, Saint Bonaventure – they died in the same year, 1274 – was less influenced by Aristotle and remained truer to the Augustinian tradition. His most celebrated treatise, *The Ascent of the Mind to God*, is Platonic in inspiration.

---

[6](Article 4).
[7]B. Davies, *The Thought of Thomas Aquinas*, p. 374.
[8]J. Ratzinger, *On the nature and mission of theology*, p. 16.

BIBLIOGRAPHY

Primary sources

Aeschylus, *The Agamemnon*, trans. A. H. Sommerstein (Loeb Classical Library, Harvard University Press, 2001)
— *The Persians*, trans. A. H. Sommerstein (Loeb Classical Library, Harvard University Press, 2001)
Alcinous [aka Albinus] *The Handbook of Platonism*, trans. J. Dillon (Clarendon Press, 1993)
Anselm, *Proslogion*, trans. M. J. Charlesworth (Clarendon Press, 1965)
Apuleius of Madaura, *On Plato and His Teaching*
Aquinas, *Summa Theologia* (Blackfriars, 1970)
Aristotle, *Metaphysics*, 2 vols, trans. H. Tredennick (Loeb Classical Library, Harvard University Press, 1933, 1935)
— *Nichomachaen Ethics*, trans. H. Rackham (Loeb Classical Library, Harvard University Press, 1926)
— *On the Soul*, trans. W. S. Hett (Loeb Classical Library, Harvard University Press, 1957)
Athanasius, *On the Incarnation*, trans. F. L. Cross (Mowbray, 1982)
— *The Orations of St Athansius Against the Arians* (Griffith, Farran, 1889)
Athenagoras, *Embassy Oxford Early Christian Texts* (Clarendon Press, 1972)
Augustine, *City of God*, 7 vols (Loeb Classical Library, Harvard University Press, 1957, 1960, 1963, 1965, 1966, 1968, 1972), trans. H. Bettenson (Penguin Classics, 2003)
— *Confessions*, 2 vols (Loeb Classical Library, Harvard University Press, 1912)
— *Confessions*, trans. A. C. Outler (SCM, 1955), also trans. H. Chadwick (OUP, 1991)
— *On Christian*, trans. M. O'Connell (New York: New City Press, 2005)
— *On Free Choice of the Will*, trans. T. Williams (Indianapolis, IN: Hackett, 1993)
— *On the Trinity*, trans. E. Hill, O.P. (New City Press, 1991)

— *On True Religion*
— *Soliloquies*
Basil, *Against Eunomius*, vols I and II, Sources Chrétiennes (1982, 1983)
— *Letters*, 3 vols (Budé, Paris, 1957, 1961, 1966)
— *On the Holy Spirit* (SVP, 1980)
Cicero, *On the Nature of the Gods*, trans. H. Rackham (Loeb Classical
    Library, Harvard University Press, 1933)
Clement, *Exhortation to the Greeks*
— of Alexandria, *Stromata*
— of Rome, *Letter to the Corinthians*
Cyril, *Second Letter to Nestorius* 219 Creeds, Councils and Controversies
    SPCK 1960
Denis the Areopagite, *The Divine Names* Classics of Western Spirituality
    (SPCK, London, 1987)
Diogenes Laertius, *Lives of the Philosophers*, 2 vols, trans. R. D. Hicks
    (Loeb Classical Library, Harvard University Press, 1925)
Epictetus, *Discourses*, 2 vols, trans. W. A. Oldfather (Loeb Classical
    Library, Harvard University Press, 1925, 1928)
Epiphanius, *Panarion*
Eunapius, *Lives of the Philosophers*, trans. W. C. Wright (Loeb Classical
    Library, Harvard University Press, 1921)
Eunomius, *Apology* in Basil, *Against Eunomius*, vol. 2, Sources
    Chrétiennes
Eusebius, *Preparation for the Gospel*
— *Ecclesiastical History*, 2 vols, trans. K. Lake and J. E. L. Oulton (Loeb
    Classical Library, Harvard University Press, 1926, 1932)
Gregory of Nazianzus, *Funeral Oration on Basil* Oration 43
— *Letters* 2 volumes, edited by P. Gallay (Budé, Paris, 1964, 1967)
— *The Theological Orations*, edited by A. I. Mason, Cambridge 1899
Gregory of Nyssa, *Catechetical Oration*, trans. J. H. Strawley (Cambridge
    University Press, 2009)
— *Contra Eunomium*
— *Life of Moses* (Paulist Press, 1978)
— *Refutatio Confessions Eunomii*
Ignatius of Antioch, *Letters*
Irenaeus, *Against the Heresies*
— *Demonstration*
Jerome, *On Illustrious Men*
Josephus, *The Jewish War*, 3 vols, trans. H. St. J. Thackeray (Loeb
    Classical Library, Harvard University Press, 1927, 1928)
Justin Martyr, *Dialogue with Trypho the Jew*
— *First Apology*
Libanius, *Oration 30*
Lies, L., *Origenes' peri archon* (Darmstadt, 1992)

Marcus Aurelius, *Meditations*, trans. C. R. Haines (Loeb Classical Library, Harvard University Press, 1916)

Nemesius, *On Human Nature*, edited by M. Morana (Teubner, 1987)

Origen, *Contra Celsum*, trans. H. Chadwick (CUP, 1965, 1980)

— *On First Principles* (Darmstadt, 1985)

— *On Prayer*, trans. by Alistair Stewart-Sykes (SVP, 2002)

Paschal, *Pensées* (Penguin Classics, 1995)

Philo, *On the Creation of the World*

Plato, *Cratylus*, trans. H. N. Fowler (Loeb Classical Library, Harvard University Press, 1926)

— *Gorgias*, trans. W. R. M. Lamb (Loeb Classical Library, Harvard University Press, 1925)

— *Parmenides*, trans. H. N. Fowler (Loeb Classical Library, Harvard University Press, 1926)

— *Phaedo*, trans. H. N. Fowler (Loeb Classical Library, Harvard University Press, 1914)

— *Protagoras*, trans. W. R. M. Lamb (Loeb Classical Library, Harvard University Press, 1924)

— *Republic*, 2 vols, trans. P. Shorey (Loeb Classical Library, Harvard University Press, 1930, 1935)

— *Symposium*, trans. W. R. M. Lamb (Loeb Classical Library, Harvard University Press, 1925)

— *Theaetetus*, trans. H. N. Fowler (Loeb Classical Library, Harvard University Press, 1921)

— *Timaeus*, trans. R. G. Bury (Loeb Classical Library, Harvard University Press, 1929)

Pliny, *Letters*, trans. W. Melmoth, 2 vols (Loeb Classical Library, Harvard University Press, 1947)

Plotinus, *Enneads*, 7 vols, trans. A. H. Armstrong (Loeb Classical Library, Harvard University Press, 1969, 1966, 1967, 1984, 1984, 1988, 1988)

Porphyry, *Against the Christians*

— *Letters*

— *Life of Plotinus*, trans. A. H. Armstrong (Loeb Classical Library, Harvard University Press, 1969)

Possidius, *Life of Augustine*

Proclus, *The Elements of Theology*, edited by E.R. Dodd (OUP, 1971)

Sallutsios, *On the Gods and the World*, edited by Gabriel Rochefort (Paris, 1996)

Seneca, *Epistles*, 3 vols, trans. R. M. Gummere (Loeb Classical Library, Harvard University Press, 1917, 1920, 1925)

Sophocles, *Oedipus Rex*

— *The Philocetes*

Suetonius, 'Life of Nero', in *Lives of the Caesars*, 2 vols, trans. J. C. Rolfe (Loeb Classical Library, Harvard University Press, 1914)

Synesius, Letter 105
Tacitus, *Annals*, 2 vols, trans. J. Jackson (Loeb Classical Library, Harvard
    University Press, 1937)
— *Histories*, 2 vols, trans. C. H. Moore (Loeb Classical Library, Harvard
    University Press, 1925, 1931)
Tatian, *Oratio ad Graecos*
Tertullian, *Against Praxeas*
— *Apology*
— *On the Flesh of Christ*
— *On the Incarnation*
— *On the Prescription of Heretics*
— *On the Soul*
— *On the Veiling of Virgins*

Secondary sources

Annas, J., 'Classical Greek Philosophy', in J. Boardman, J. Griffin, and
    O. Murray (eds), *Oxford History of Greece and the Hellenistic World*
    (Oxford University Press, 1991)
Arnold, M., *Literature and Dogma* (London, 1883, 1904)
Bigg, C., *The Christian Platonists of Alexandria: The 1886 Bampton
    Lectures* (Oxford University Press, 1913)
Braudel, F., *The Mediterranean in the Ancient World* (Allen Lane, 2001)
Chadwick, H., *Early Christian Thought and the Classical Tradition:
    Studies in Justin, Clement and Origen* (Oxford University Press, 1984)
— *East and West, The Making of a Rift in the Church* (Oxford University
    Press, 2003)
— *Eucharist and Christology in the Nestorian Controversy* (JTS, 1951)
— *The Church in Ancient Society* (Oxford University Press, 2001)
Clark, E., *The Origenist Controversy* (Princeton University Press, 1993)
Copleston, F. C., *Aquinas: An Introduction to the Life and Work of the
    Great Medieval Thinker* (Penguin Books, 1991)
Crouzel, H., *Origène et la philosophie* (Paris, 1963)
Davies, D., *The Thought of Thomas Aquinas* (Clarendon Paperbacks, 1993)
Dihle, A., *The Theory of Will in Classical Antiquity* (University of
    California Press, 1992)
Dodds, E. R., *Elements of Theology of Proclus* (Oxford University Press,
    1963)
— *Pagans and Christians in an Age of Anxiety* (Cambridge University
    Press, 1965)
Doerries, H. *Gregory von Nyssa und die* philospphie (Brill, 1976)

Edwards, M., *Origen Against Plato* (Ashgate Publishing, 2002)

Field, R., *Of the Church* (Cambridge University Press, 1847)

Gibbon, E., *The History of the Decline and fall of the Roman Empire*, 6 vols (Everyman, 1994)

Gregg and Groh, *Early Arianism: A View of Salvation* (Fortress, 1981)

Hanson, R. P. C., *The Search for the Christian Doctrine of God: The Arian Controversy 318–381 AD* (T&T Clark, 1988)

Hatch, E., *The Influence of Greek Ideas and Usages upon the Christian Church, Hibbert Lectures 1888* (Williams and Norgate, 1907)

Heil, G. and Ritter, A. M. (eds), *Corpus Dionysiacum* (Gottingen, 1990)

Hengel, M., *The 'Hellenization' of Judaea in the First Century AD* (London, 1989)

Hopkins, K., *A World Full of Gods: Pagans, Jews and Christians in the Roman Empire* (Weidenfeld and Nicolson, 1999)

— *A World Full of Gods: The Strange Triumph of Christianity* (The Free Press, 2000)

Inge, W. R., *The Church and the Age* (Longmans, 1912)

Kelly, J. N. D. *Golden Mouth: The Story of John Chrysostom* (Duckworth & Co., 1996)

Lancel, S., *Saint Augustine* (E. T. SCM Press, 1999)

Marinus, *Life of Proclus (412–485)* (Phanes Press, 1987)

May, G., *Schopfung aus dem Nichts* (Berlin, 1978)

Merlan, *The Cambridge History of Later Greek and Early Mediaeval Philosophy* (Cambridge University Press, 1967)

Newman, *An Essay in Favour of a Grammar of Assent* (1870)

— *Apologia pro vita sua*

Pohlenz, M., *Vom Zorne Gottes [On the Anger of God]* (1909)

Pope John Paul II, *Fides et ratio* (Catholic Truth Society, 1988)

Powell, J. U. (ed.), *Collectanea Alexandrina*

Prosper Alfaric, *L'évolution intellectuelle de Saint Augustin* (Paris, 1918)

Ratzinger, J., *The Nature and Mission of Theology* (Ignatius Press, 1995)

Rist and Markus, *History of Late Greek and Early Mediaeval Philosophy*

Sanders, E. P., *Paul: A Very Short Introduction* (Oxford University Press, 2001)

Sozomenus, *Ecclesiastical History: A History of the Church in Nine Books, from A.D. 324 to A.D. 440* (Nabu Press, 2010)

Stead, C., *Divine Substance* (Oxford University Press, 1977)

— *The Platonism of Arius* (JTS, 1964)

von Campenhausen, H., *The Fathers of the Latin Church* (Stanford University Press, 1964) von Harnack, A., *The Essence of Christianity* (1900–1) (Karl Holl, 1866–1926)

Wiles, M. F., 'Eunomius: hair splitting dialectician and defender of the accessibility of salvation', in Rowan Williams (ed.), *Essays in honour of Henry Chadwick* (Cambridge, 1982)

Williams, R., *Arius, Heresy and Tradition* (Darton, Longman and Todd, 1987)

— *The Wound of Knowledge* (Darton, Longman and Todd, 1979)

Wilson, N., 'Introduction', in *Historical Miscellany*, Aelien (Loeb Classical Library, Harvard University Press, 1997)

Aristotle, *Later Analytics*

Rist, J. M., *Augustine: Ancient Thought Baptized* (Cambridge University Press, 1994, p. 45)

INDEX